"Coding Creativity: How to Build a Chatbot or Art Generator from Scratch."

Coding Creativity - How to build A Chatbot or Art Generator from Scratch with Bonus: The Ai Prompting Bible

Michael Ferguson

Published by Michael Ferguson, 2023.

CODING CREATIVITY - HOW TO BUILD A CHATBOT OR ART GENERATOR FROM SCRATCH WITH BONUS: THE AI PROMPTING BIBLE

First edition. April 17, 2023.

ISBN: 979-8215402252

Written by Michael Ferguson.

As I embark on this journey of explaining the technical intricacies of building a chatbot from scratch, I am reminded of the words of the esteemed Arthur C. Clarke, the renowned British science fiction author. He once said, "Any sufficiently advanced technology is indistinguishable from magic." And indeed, building a chatbot is a marvel of modern technology, where code and creativity converge to create an interactive, intelligent conversational experience that can captivate users and leave them spellbound.

The canvas on which we shall paint our technical masterpiece is a blank slate, a realm of possibilities waiting to be unlocked. But fear not, for I shall be your guide on this exciting quest, as we delve into the inner workings of building a chatbot that can hold its own in the realm of human conversation.

The foundation of any chatbot lies in its ability to understand and respond to user input. This requires a keen understanding of natural language processing (NLP), the branch of artificial intelligence (AI) that focuses on enabling computers to understand and process human language. NLP is the key that unlocks the door to meaningful conversation between humans and machines, and it is the first brick that we shall lay in our technical edifice.

To build a chatbot, we must first gather the necessary tools of the trade. One such tool is a programming language, which serves as the medium through which we shall craft our bot's intelligence. There are several programming languages that are commonly used in the realm of chatbot development, each with its own strengths and weaknesses. Python, with its rich ecosystem of NLP libraries such as NLTK, SpaCy, and TensorFlow, is a popular choice due to its ease of use and versatility. Java, with its robustness and scalability, is also a formidable contender. Other languages like C++, JavaScript, and Ruby can also be wielded with skill and finesse, depending on the requirements of the chatbot.

Once we have chosen our programming language, we must gather our allies in the form of libraries and frameworks that will aid us in our quest. These tools are the building blocks that will allow us to construct our chatbot with precision and efficiency. Some notable libraries and frameworks in the field of NLP include:

Natural Language Toolkit (NLTK): This comprehensive library for Python provides a wide range of tools for tasks such as tokenization, part-of-speech tagging, and named entity recognition, making it a powerful weapon in the NLP arsenal.

SpaCy: Another popular NLP library for Python, SpaCy offers advanced features such as named entity recognition, dependency parsing, and word vectors, making it a formidable ally in the battle for chatbot supremacy.

TensorFlow: This powerful machine learning framework, developed by Google, provides a range of tools for building and training deep neural networks, making it an invaluable asset for creating chatbots with advanced capabilities such as sentiment analysis and language generation.

Dialogflow: This conversational AI platform, powered by Google Cloud, provides tools for building chatbots with natural language understanding (NLU) and natural language generation (NLG) capabilities, making it a compelling choice for chatbot development.

Rasa: This open-source conversational AI framework provides tools for building chatbots with advanced features such as intent recognition, dialogue management, and slot filling, making it a potent weapon in the chatbot arsenal.

Armed with our chosen programming language and the tools of our trade, we must now embark on the arduous task of training our chatbot's brain. NLP models require training data to learn from, and this data is the fuel that powers our chatbot's intelligence. Our training data shall be the corpus of human language, a vast ocean of words, phrases, and expressions that provide the raw material for our chatbot to learn and understand.

To train our chatbot, we shall follow a two-step process: pre-processing and modeling. Pre-processing involves cleaning and transforming raw text data into a format that can be fed into our NLP models. This includes tasks such as tokenization, where we split text into individual words or phrases, and removing stop words, which are common words like "the" and "and" that do not carry much meaning. We may also perform tasks such as lemmatization, where we reduce words to their root form, and entity recognition, where we identify and label specific entities such as names, dates, and locations.

Once our data is pre-processed, we can move on to the modeling phase. This is where the true magic of NLP happens, as we train our models to understand and generate human-like language. One popular approach is to use machine learning algorithms, such as supervised learning, unsupervised learning, or deep learning, to train our models. Supervised learning involves training our models on labeled data, where we have input text data paired with corresponding output labels. Unsupervised learning, on the other hand, involves training our models on unlabeled data, where the model must learn to recognize patterns and structures in the data without any pre-defined labels. Deep learning, a subfield of machine learning, involves training neural networks with multiple hidden layers to learn complex patterns and representations from the data.

Another approach is to use rule-based techniques, where we define a set of rules or patterns for the chatbot to follow. For example, we may define rules such as "If the user asks about the weather, respond with the current weather information." or "If the user mentions a specific product, provide information about that product." These rules are handcrafted and can be designed to handle specific scenarios, but may require regular updates to keep up with changing language patterns and user expectations.

As our models learn and improve over time, we must also ensure that our chatbot can engage in meaningful dialogue with users. This requires a robust dialogue management system that can handle the flow of conversation, maintain context, and generate appropriate responses. Dialogue management involves techniques such as intent recognition, where we identify the user's intention based on their input, and slot filling, where we extract relevant information from the user's input to carry out the conversation. We may also implement a memory mechanism, where the chatbot can store and recall past interactions to provide a personalized experience.

Once our chatbot is trained and equipped with a robust dialogue management system, we must put it to the test. Testing is a critical phase in the chatbot development process, as it allows us to identify and fix any issues or shortcomings in our bot's performance. We can conduct various types of tests, such as unit testing, integration testing, and user acceptance testing, to ensure that our chatbot is functioning as intended and providing a seamless user experience. We may also leverage techniques such as A/B testing, where we compare the performance of different versions of our chatbot to optimize its performance.

But our quest does not end with testing. As technology evolves and language patterns change, our chatbot must continue to learn and adapt to stay relevant. This requires continuous improvement and maintenance, as we update our training data, refine our models, and enhance our dialogue management system to keep our chatbot sharp and responsive. We must also listen to user feedback and iterate on our chatbot's performance, taking into account user preferences and expectations to ensure that our chatbot remains a trusted and engaging conversational companion.

As I reflect on this awe-inspiring journey of building a chatbot from scratch, I am reminded of the words of the legendary J.R.R. Tolkien, who once wrote, "All that is gold does not glitter, not all those who wander are lost." Building a chatbot may not always be a smooth ride, with its challenges and complexities, but the end result is truly golden. The ability to create a machine that can understand and respond to human language is a remarkable feat of technological innovation.

In the midst of the technical intricacies and complexities, there is also an artistic aspect to building a chatbot. Just like an author crafts a story with carefully chosen words and phrases to captivate the reader's imagination, a chatbot developer crafts a conversational experience by choosing the right algorithms, techniques, and data to create a seamless and engaging interaction with users. It requires creativity, intuition, and a deep understanding of human language to build a chatbot that can hold a conversation with fluidity and coherence.

The journey of building a chatbot from scratch is not without its challenges. One of the biggest challenges is data. Data is the fuel that powers our chatbot, and having high-quality and diverse data is crucial for training our models to understand and generate human-like language. Obtaining and curating large datasets, especially in specialized domains, can be time-consuming and resource-intensive. We may need to clean, preprocess, and augment the data to ensure its accuracy and relevance. We may also encounter issues with data bias, where the data used for training may introduce biases that can affect the chatbot's responses. Addressing these challenges requires careful consideration and attention to detail, just like a master wordsmith carefully crafts each word to create a compelling narrative.

Another challenge is the complexity of natural language itself. Language is a rich and dynamic system that is constantly evolving, with nuances, idioms, and cultural references that can pose difficulties for a chatbot to understand and respond to accurately. For instance, language is contextual, and the same words can have different meanings depending on the context in which they are used. Sarcasm, irony, and humor are also aspects of language that can be particularly challenging for a chatbot to interpret. Additionally, users may have different speaking styles, accents, and dialects that the chatbot must be able to understand and adapt to. Just like a skilled author masterfully weaves language to create a vivid and immersive story, a chatbot developer must navigate the complexities of language to create a chatbot that can converse with users in a natural and meaningful way.

Another key challenge is dialogue management. A chatbot must be able to understand the user's intent, remember past interactions, and generate appropriate responses to maintain a coherent conversation. This requires sophisticated dialogue management techniques that can handle the flow of conversation, keep track of context, and generate responses that are relevant and coherent. Dialogue management is like the plot of a story, guiding the conversation and ensuring that the chatbot and the user are on the same page.

The advancements in technology, particularly in the field of deep learning, have greatly advanced the capabilities of chatbots. Deep learning models such as recurrent neural networks (RNNs) and transformers have shown impressive performance in tasks such as language modeling, sequence generation, and sentiment analysis, which are fundamental to building a chatbot. These models can learn from large amounts of data, capture complex patterns in language, and generate coherent responses that are indistinguishable from those of a human. However, training and fine-tuning these models require substantial computational resources, expertise, and experimentation to achieve optimal performance. It is like the use of vivid and descriptive language by a skilled author to create a compelling narrative that captivates the reader's imagination.

Once our chatbot is trained and ready, we can deploy it to a suitable platform or framework that allows it to interact with users. This could be a website, a messaging app, a voice assistant, or any other platform where users can engage with the chatbot. Deployment requires careful consideration of factors such as scalability, security, and performance. Just like an author publishes their story in a book, the deployment of a chatbot is the final step in bringing it to life and making it accessible to users.

Scalability is an important consideration in building a chatbot, as it needs to be able to handle a large number of users and conversations simultaneously without sacrificing performance. This requires choosing the right architecture and infrastructure that can scale horizontally, meaning it can handle increased loads by adding more resources, such as servers or containers, as needed. This is similar to how a successful author's book may become widely popular and attract a large audience, requiring more copies to be printed to meet the demand.

Security is another critical aspect of chatbot development. Chatbots may handle sensitive user information, such as personal data or payment details, and must ensure the confidentiality, integrity, and availability of this data. Implementing robust security measures, such as data encryption, authentication, and authorization, is essential to protect users' privacy and prevent any potential security breaches. It is akin to how a bestselling author may take measures to protect their manuscript from unauthorized access to prevent any leaks or breaches of confidentiality.

Performance is also crucial in building a chatbot that provides a seamless and smooth user experience. Users expect quick and accurate responses from a chatbot, and any delays or lags in the system can lead to frustration and dissatisfaction. Optimizing the chatbot's performance, such as reducing response time and minimizing computational overhead, is essential to deliver a responsive and efficient conversational experience. This is similar to how an author may spend time editing and polishing their manuscript to ensure that it flows smoothly and captivates the reader's attention without any hiccups.

In addition to scalability, security, and performance, monitoring and maintenance are ongoing tasks in the life cycle of a chatbot. Just like an author may need to revise and update their story as new information or feedback becomes available, a chatbot requires continuous monitoring and maintenance to ensure its accuracy, relevance, and effectiveness. This may involve analyzing user interactions, identifying areas for improvement, and updating the chatbot's responses or algorithms accordingly. It may also require regular updates to the underlying technology stack, such as libraries, APIs, or frameworks, to ensure that the chatbot remains up-to-date with the latest advancements in the field of natural language processing and machine learning. Monitoring and maintenance are crucial to keeping the chatbot's performance at its peak, just like an author's dedication to constantly improving their writing skills to create captivating stories that stand the test of time.

One of the exciting aspects of building a chatbot is the opportunity to customize and personalize the conversation for different users. Just like an author may use different writing styles or tones depending on the target audience or genre, a chatbot can be tailored to specific users or domains. This involves incorporating domain-specific knowledge or context into the chatbot's responses to make them more relevant and meaningful to the users. For instance, a customer service chatbot for a fashion brand may need to understand fashion-specific terms and trends, while a medical chatbot may require knowledge of medical conditions and treatments. Personalizing the conversation can greatly enhance the user experience and create a more engaging and immersive interaction, similar to how an author may use different writing techniques or genres to resonate with different readers.

Another interesting aspect of chatbot development is the integration with external services or APIs. Just like an author may use references or citations from other sources to enrich their story, a chatbot can leverage external services or APIs to provide additional functionality or information to the users. For example, a weather chatbot may integrate with a weather API to provide real-time weather updates, or a booking chatbot may integrate with a booking API to facilitate reservation requests. Integrating external services or APIs requires careful consideration of API integration protocols, data formats, authentication, and error handling to ensure smooth communication between the chatbot and the external services. It may also involve handling potential errors or exceptions that may occur during the API calls, and providing meaningful error messages to users. This integration can greatly expand the capabilities of the chatbot, making it a powerful tool for users to access a wide range of services or information in a seamless and convenient manner.

Furthermore, building a chatbot from scratch also involves designing the conversation flow and user interface (UI). Just like an author carefully crafts the plot and character interactions in their story, a chatbot's conversation flow must be well-designed to provide a natural and intuitive conversational experience. This involves defining the different intents or purposes of user inputs, creating appropriate responses, and handling potential user queries or requests in a conversational manner. The chatbot's UI, whether it's a text-based interface or a voice-based interface, must also be designed with usability in mind, ensuring that users can easily interact with the chatbot and understand its responses.

Designing the conversation flow and UI of a chatbot requires a deep understanding of user behavior, language patterns, and conversational dynamics. It may involve using techniques from human-computer interaction (HCI), natural language processing (NLP), and user experience (UX) design to create an engaging and enjoyable conversation for users. Just like an author crafts their story to capture the reader's imagination and emotions, a well-designed chatbot conversation can create a memorable and immersive experience for users, keeping them engaged and coming back for more interactions.

Finally, testing and evaluation are crucial steps in building a chatbot to ensure its accuracy, reliability, and effectiveness. Just like an author may undergo multiple rounds of editing and proofreading to catch any errors or inconsistencies in their story, a chatbot must undergo rigorous testing to identify and fix any issues before it is deployed to users. This may involve different types of testing, such as unit testing, integration testing, and user acceptance testing, to verify the chatbot's functionality, performance, and usability. It may also involve evaluating the chatbot's performance against predefined metrics, such as response time, accuracy, and user satisfaction, to ensure that it meets the desired quality standards.

Testing and evaluation are iterative processes that may involve multiple rounds of feedback, analysis, and refinement. Just like an author may receive feedback from beta readers or editors to improve their story, a chatbot may receive feedback from users or stakeholders to identify areas for improvement. This feedback loop is essential to continuously enhance the chatbot's performance and ensure that it meets the evolving needs and expectations of users.

In conclusion, building a chatbot from scratch requires a multidisciplinary approach, combining technical expertise in natural language processing, machine learning, software engineering, and user experience design. It involves several stages, including defining the chatbot's purpose and scope, collecting and preparing data, training and fine-tuning machine learning models, integrating external services, designing the conversation flow and UI, and testing and evaluating the chatbot's performance. Just like an author puts their heart and soul into crafting a compelling story, building a chatbot is a labor of love that requires creativity, technical skill, and attention to detail to create a conversational experience that is engaging, efficient, and enjoyable for users.

As I reflect on the technical side of building a chatbot from scratch, I am filled with a sense of awe and wonder. Just like an author weaves words into a masterpiece, a chatbot is crafted through a symphony of algorithms, data, and human-computer interaction principles. It is a testament to the marvels of modern technology, where machines are empowered with the ability to understand and respond to human language, transcending the boundaries of traditional human-computer interaction.

The journey of building a chatbot from scratch is akin to a thrilling adventure, filled with challenges, discoveries, and moments of triumph. It requires the deft hands of a skilled engineer, the keen eye of a meticulous data scientist, and the creative mind of a UX designer, all working in harmony to bring the chatbot to life.

Just like an author starts with a blank canvas, a chatbot begins with a vision and a purpose. The first step in building a chatbot is to define its purpose and scope. This involves understanding the specific tasks or functions the chatbot is intended to perform, and the target audience it is designed to serve. Is it a customer service chatbot for a website, a virtual assistant to help with scheduling appointments, or a language tutor to assist with learning? Clarifying the chatbot's purpose and scope is essential to guide the subsequent technical decisions and ensure that the chatbot aligns with the desired goals.

Once the purpose and scope are defined, the next step in building a chatbot is to collect and prepare the data. Just like an author researches and gathers information for their story, a chatbot relies on data to understand and respond to user inputs. This data may come from various sources, such as customer interactions, user queries, or external databases. It needs to be collected, cleaned, and structured in a format that can be easily processed by machine learning algorithms.

Data preparation is a critical step in building a chatbot, as the quality and relevance of the data directly impact the chatbot's performance. The data must be cleansed of any inconsistencies, errors, or irrelevant information that may adversely affect the chatbot's accuracy and reliability. It may also need to be annotated or labeled to create a supervised learning dataset for training machine learning models.

Once the data is prepared, the next step is to train and fine-tune machine learning models. Just like an author carefully crafts the characters and dialogues in their story, a chatbot's models are trained on the prepared data to learn patterns and relationships between user inputs and appropriate responses. This typically involves using techniques from natural language processing (NLP) and machine learning, such as supervised learning, unsupervised learning, or reinforcement learning.

Supervised learning is commonly used in chatbot development to train models on labeled data, where the correct responses are provided during training. The models learn to map user inputs to appropriate responses based on the patterns observed in the labeled data. Unsupervised learning may also be used to discover patterns or groupings in the data without labeled examples, and reinforcement learning may be employed to enable the chatbot to learn from feedback provided by users during interactions.

Training and fine-tuning machine learning models require iterative experimentation, evaluation, and refinement. Just like an author revises and edits their story to improve its coherence and flow, a chatbot's models are continuously tweaked and refined to enhance their accuracy, robustness, and performance. This may involve experimenting with different algorithms, feature engineering techniques, or hyperparameter tuning to optimize the models for the chatbot's specific purpose and domain.

Once the models are trained and fine-tuned, the next step is to integrate the chatbot with external services, databases, or APIs. Just like an author may reference external sources or research to enrich their story, a chatbot may need to access external services to provide accurate and up-to-date information to users. This may involve integrating with APIs (Application Programming Interfaces) of external services, such as weather APIs, news APIs, or social media APIs, to fetch relevant data or perform actions on behalf of users.

Integration with external services requires technical expertise in handling integration protocols, data formats, authentication, and error handling to ensure smooth communication between the chatbot and the external services. It may also involve handling potential errors or exceptions that may occur during the integration process, such as handling API timeouts, errors in data retrieval, or authentication failures.

Once the chatbot is integrated with external services, the next step is to design its user interface and user experience (UI/UX). Just like an author carefully crafts the layout, fonts, and colors of their book, a chatbot's UI/UX plays a crucial role in its usability and user satisfaction. The chatbot's interface should be intuitive, visually appealing, and easy to use, with clear prompts and instructions for users to interact with.

The UI/UX design should also consider the context in which the chatbot will be used, such as the device (e.g., mobile, web, smart speaker), the platform (e.g., Facebook Messenger, WhatsApp, Slack), and the target audience's preferences and behaviors. It should be responsive, accessible, and compatible with different devices and platforms, providing a seamless experience for users across various touchpoints.

Once the UI/UX design is finalized, the next step is to implement the chatbot's front-end and back-end functionalities. Just like an author writes the story and brings it to life with characters, dialogues, and settings, a chatbot's front-end and back-end work together to enable interactions with users.

The front-end of a chatbot typically involves the development of the user interface, including the visual design, user prompts, input fields, buttons, and other interactive elements. It may also include the development of conversation flows, where the chatbot guides users through a series of interactions to collect input, provide responses, and fulfill tasks.

The back-end of a chatbot involves the development of the logic and functionality that powers the chatbot's responses and actions. This may include the integration with machine learning models, handling user inputs, processing and analyzing data, generating responses, and managing conversations. The back-end also needs to handle error handling, exception handling, and maintaining context across multiple turns of the conversation.

Developing the front-end and back-end of a chatbot requires expertise in programming languages, frameworks, libraries, and tools, depending on the chosen technology stack. Popular programming languages for chatbot development include Python, JavaScript, Java, or C#, and there are various frameworks and libraries available for NLP, machine learning, and chatbot development, such as TensorFlow, PyTorch, Dialogflow, or Rasa.

Once the front-end and back-end of the chatbot are developed, the next step is to test and debug the chatbot thoroughly. Just like an author proofreads and edits their story for grammar, spelling, and coherence, a chatbot needs to be thoroughly tested for its accuracy, reliability, and performance.

Testing a chatbot involves multiple stages, including unit testing, integration testing, and user acceptance testing. Unit testing involves testing individual components of the chatbot, such as the machine learning models, APIs, or UI elements, to ensure they function as intended. Integration testing involves testing the interactions between different components of the chatbot, such as the front-end and back-end, to ensure seamless communication and integration. User acceptance testing involves testing the chatbot with real users to gather feedback and ensure it meets the intended purpose and expectations.

During testing, any bugs, errors, or inconsistencies that are identified need to be addressed and fixed promptly. This may involve debugging the code, refining the models, or refining the conversation flows. It requires meticulous attention to detail and thorough testing to ensure that the chatbot performs optimally and delivers a seamless experience to users.

Once the chatbot has been thoroughly tested and refined, and all the identified issues have been addressed, it is ready for deployment. Just like an author publishes their book for readers to enjoy, a chatbot is deployed to the chosen platform or channels, such as a website, a messaging platform, a mobile app, or a smart speaker, for users to interact with.

Deployment of a chatbot involves setting up the necessary infrastructure, configuring the hosting environment, and ensuring the chatbot is accessible to users. Depending on the chosen technology stack, the deployment process may involve deploying the front-end and back-end components separately or as a unified system. It may also involve setting up security measures, such as authentication and encryption, to protect user data and ensure the chatbot's security.

Once the chatbot is deployed, it is important to monitor its performance and gather feedback from users. Just like an author listens to readers' feedback and reviews to improve their writing, monitoring and feedback play a crucial role in continuously enhancing the chatbot's performance and user satisfaction.

Monitoring the chatbot involves tracking its usage, performance, and errors. This may include monitoring user interactions, response times, error rates, and other performance metrics. Feedback from users can be collected through surveys, user reviews, or feedback forms, and can provide valuable insights into the chatbot's strengths, weaknesses, and areas for improvement.

Based on the monitoring and feedback, the chatbot may require updates, enhancements, or bug fixes. These updates may involve refining the conversation flows, updating the machine learning models, improving the UI/UX, or integrating new features. It requires continuous improvement and iteration to keep the chatbot up-to-date, relevant, and effective in meeting the users' needs.

In addition to monitoring and feedback, it is also essential to keep the chatbot secure and compliant with relevant regulations and policies. Just like an author ensures their book adheres to copyright laws and publishing guidelines, a chatbot needs to comply with data privacy regulations, security standards, and other legal requirements.

This may involve implementing measures such as data encryption, user authentication, access controls, and regular security audits. It also requires staying up-to-date with the latest regulations, policies, and best practices in the field of chatbot development and making necessary adjustments to ensure compliance.

Building a chatbot from scratch is a complex and challenging process that requires expertise in various technical skills, including natural language processing, machine learning, programming, and software development. It also requires creativity, problem-solving skills, attention to detail, and continuous improvement mindset to create a chatbot that delivers a compelling user experience.

All in all, the rewards of building a chatbot can be immense. Just like an author's book can captivate readers and leave a lasting impact, a well-designed and well-implemented chatbot can engage users, streamline processes, provide personalized assistance, and enhance customer experience. From customer service and support, to sales and marketing, to internal processes and operations, chatbots can offer numerous benefits for businesses and users alike.

In conclusion, building a chatbot from scratch is a complex and exciting technical endeavor that involves multiple stages, from defining the purpose and scope of the chatbot, designing the conversation flows, integrating with external services, implementing front-end and back-end functionalities, testing and debugging, deploying, monitoring, and continuously improving. It requires a deep understanding of natural language processing, machine learning, programming, and software development, as well as creativity, problem-solving skills, attention to detail, and compliance with regulations and policies. Just like an author creates a story that captivates readers, a well-designed and well-implemented chatbot can engage users, streamline processes, and enhance user experience in various domains. Whether it's in customer service, sales, marketing, or internal operations, chatbots have the potential to revolutionize the way businesses interact with users, making interactions more efficient, personalized, and enjoyable. So, take up the challenge and embark on the journey of building your chatbot from scratch, and unleash the power of conversational AI to create meaningful and memorable user experiences!

Chapter 1: What are Chatbots and Ai Art Generators

Chatbots and art generators are two of the most exciting and rapidly evolving fields in technology today. These tools have the potential to revolutionize how we interact with technology, providing a more intuitive and natural way of communicating with machines and generating novel and inspiring works of art. However, before delving into the technical details of building a chatbot or art generator, it is essential to understand the basics of what these tools are and how they work. In this chapter, we will provide an overview of chatbots and art generators, explaining the different types of chatbots and approaches to generative art. Additionally, we will explore the potential applications of these tools, ranging from customer service to creating unique pieces of digital art.

What are Chatbots? A chatbot is a computer program designed to simulate human conversation, either through text or voice. Chatbots are often used in customer service and support, where they can answer frequently asked questions, resolve simple issues, and direct users to the appropriate resources. However, chatbots can also be used in a variety of other applications, such as gaming, education, and healthcare.

Types of Chatbots There are several types of chatbots, each with its strengths and weaknesses. The three most common types of chatbots are:

Rule-Based Chatbots: Rule-based chatbots are the simplest type of chatbot. They work by following a set of predefined rules and responses, which are triggered by specific keywords or phrases. Rule-based chatbots are limited in their ability to understand natural language, and they can only respond to queries that match their pre-programmed responses.

Machine Learning Chatbots: Machine learning chatbots are more advanced than rule-based chatbots. They use algorithms to learn from user interactions and improve their responses over time. Machine learning chatbots can understand natural language and context, allowing them to provide more accurate and personalized responses.

Natural Language Processing (NLP) Chatbots: NLP chatbots are the most advanced type of chatbot. They use machine learning algorithms to understand the nuances of human language, including context, sentiment, and tone. NLP chatbots can provide highly personalized and conversational responses, making them ideal for applications such as virtual assistants and customer support.

Approaches to Generative Art Generative art is a form of digital art that is created through the use of algorithms and computer programs. Generative art can take many forms, including visual art, music, and literature. There are several approaches to generative art, each with its strengths and weaknesses. The three most common approaches to generative art are:

Rule-Based Systems: Rule-based systems use a set of predefined rules and parameters to generate art. Artists can specify the rules and parameters to control the output of the system, allowing them to create highly detailed and complex works of art.

Chapter 2: Neural Networks

Neural networks are a type of machine learning algorithm that can be used to generate art. Artists can train a neural network on a dataset of existing art, and the network will then generate new pieces of art based on what it has learned. Neural networks can produce highly realistic and detailed works of art, but they can also be unpredictable and difficult to control.

Genetic Algorithms: Genetic algorithms are a type of optimization algorithm that can be used to generate art. Artists can specify a set of parameters and fitness functions, and the algorithm will then generate new pieces of art based on those parameters. Genetic algorithms can create highly diverse and unpredictable works of art, but they can also be computationally expensive and difficult to tune.

Applications of Chatbots and Art Generators Chatbots and art generators have a wide range of applications in different fields. For example:

Customer Service: Chatbots can be used to improve customer service and support by answering frequently asked questions, resolving simple issues, and directing users to the appropriate resources. Chatbots can handle a high volume of requests, freeing up human agents to focus on more complex issues.

Workflow Automation: Chatbots can also be used to automate workflows and streamline business processes. For example, chatbots can be used to schedule appointments, process orders, and track shipments.

Virtual Assistants: NLP chatbots can be used as virtual assistants, providing personalized and conversational responses to users' queries.

Virtual assistants can be used in a variety of applications, including personal productivity, home automation, and healthcare.

Art and Design: Art generators can be used to create unique and inspiring pieces of digital art. Artists and designers can use these tools to explore new forms of expression and generate novel ideas for their work.

Conclusion Chatbots and art generators are two of the most exciting and rapidly evolving fields in technology today. These tools have the potential to revolutionize how we interact with technology and generate new forms of digital art. However, before delving into the technical details of building a chatbot or art generator, it is essential to understand the basics of what these tools are and how they work. This chapter has provided an overview of chatbots and art generators, explaining the different types of chatbots and approaches to generative art. Additionally, we have explored the potential applications of these tools, ranging from customer service to creating unique pieces of digital art. In the following chapters, we will delve deeper into the technical details of building and deploying chatbots and art generators, providing practical guidance and examples along the way.

Chapter 3: Choosing the right programming language:

Choosing the right programming language is a crucial step in building a successful chatbot or art generator. The programming language you choose will have a significant impact on the ease of development and the performance of your tool. There are many programming languages to choose from, each with its own strengths and weaknesses. This chapter will provide an overview of some of the most popular programming languages used in chatbot and art generator development and provide guidance on how to select the best language for your project.

Python Python is one of the most popular programming languages used in chatbot and art generator development. It is known for its simplicity, readability, and ease of use. Python has a large community of developers and a vast library of modules and frameworks, making it a versatile and powerful tool for building chatbots and art generators.

Pros:

- Simple syntax: Python has a simple and readable syntax, making it easy to learn and write code.
- Large community: Python has a large and active community of developers, providing a wealth of resources and support.
- Large library: Python has a vast library of modules and frameworks, making it easy to build complex applications quickly.

Cons:

- Performance: Python can be slower than other programming

languages, making it less suitable for high-performance applications.

- Limited support for mobile development: Python has limited support for mobile development, making it less suitable for mobile chatbot applications.

JavaScript JavaScript is a popular programming language used in web development, including chatbot and art generator development. JavaScript is known for its flexibility and versatility, making it a popular choice for building interactive and dynamic web applications.

Pros:

- Versatility: JavaScript is a versatile language that can be used for both client-side and server-side development.
- Large community: JavaScript has a large and active community of developers, providing a wealth of resources and support.
- High-performance: JavaScript is a high-performance language that can handle large-scale applications.

Cons:

- Complexity: JavaScript can be complex and difficult to learn, especially for beginners.
- Security: JavaScript can be vulnerable to security vulnerabilities, making it important to take security precautions when building chatbots or art generators.

Java Java is a popular programming language used in a variety of applications, including chatbots and art generators. Java is known for its reliability, scalability, and security, making it a popular choice for building enterprise-level applications.

Pros:

- Reliability: Java is known for its reliability and stability, making it a popular choice for building high-performance applications.
- Scalability: Java is highly scalable, making it suitable for large-scale applications.
- Security: Java is known for its security features, making it a good choice for building secure applications.

Cons:

- Complexity: Java can be complex and difficult to learn, especially for beginners.
- Performance: Java can be slower than other programming languages, making it less suitable for high-performance applications.

Choosing the Best Programming Language for Your Project When choosing a programming language for your chatbot or art generator project, there are several factors to consider, including your project requirements, the size and complexity of your project, and your team's expertise. Here are some tips for selecting the best programming language for your project:

Consider your project requirements: Think about the functionality you want your chatbot or art generator to have and the platform you want to deploy it on. Some programming languages may be better suited for specific platforms or applications.

Assess the size and complexity of your project: Consider the size and complexity of your project when choosing a programming language. Some languages may be more suitable for small or simple projects, while others may be better for large-scale or complex applications.

Evaluate your team's expertise: Consider the experience and expertise of your development team when choosing a programming language. Choosing a language that your team is familiar with can help streamline development and improve the overall quality of the project.

Consider performance and scalability: If performance and scalability are important factors for your project, choose a language that can handle high-performance applications and can scale to meet your needs.

Research available resources and support: Consider the availability of resources and support for the programming language you are considering. A language with a large and active community of developers and a vast library of modules and frameworks can make development easier and more efficient.

Choosing the right programming language is an important decision when building a chatbot or art generator. The programming language you choose will have a significant impact on the ease of development and the performance of your tool. Python, JavaScript, and Java are some of the most popular programming languages used in chatbot and art generator development, each with its own strengths and weaknesses. When choosing a programming language, consider your project requirements, the size and complexity of your project, your team's expertise, and the availability of resources and support. With careful consideration, you can choose the best programming language for your chatbot or art generator project and build a successful tool that meets your needs.

Chapter 4: Designing You User Interface – The Front End

When designing a chatbot or art generator, creating a user-friendly interface is essential to ensure that users can interact with your tool effectively. A well-designed interface can help users navigate your tool, understand how to use it, and enjoy the experience of creating or interacting with it. This chapter will explore the principles of user interface design, provide guidance on selecting the best design tools for your project and offer tips on how to test and refine your user interface design.

Principles of User Interface Design When designing a user interface, there are several principles to keep in mind to ensure that your tool is easy to use, effective, and enjoyable for your users.

Keep it simple and intuitive: Your interface should be simple and intuitive, with clear and easy-to-understand instructions. Avoid cluttering your interface with unnecessary features or elements that can confuse or overwhelm your users.

Use visual hierarchy: Use visual hierarchy to help users navigate your interface and prioritize the most important elements. This can include using contrasting colors, larger fonts, or bold typography to draw attention to key elements.

Incorporate interactive elements: Incorporate interactive elements, such as buttons, sliders, or animations, to make your interface more engaging and user-friendly. These elements can help users navigate your tool, provide feedback, and improve the overall user experience.

Ensure accessibility: Ensure that your interface is accessible for users with different needs, such as those with visual or hearing impairments.

This can include using appropriate color contrast, providing alternative text for images and offering keyboard navigation options.

Design Tools for User Interface Design There are several design tools available that can help you create an effective user interface for your chatbot or art generator project. These tools can help you design your interface, create mockups, and test your design before you begin development.

Sketch: Sketch is a popular design tool that is used by many designers to create user interfaces. It offers a range of features, such as vector editing, design libraries, and collaboration tools, making it a versatile tool for UI design.

Figma: Figma is a cloud-based design tool that allows designers to create and share their work in real-time. It offers a range of features, such as prototyping, design systems, and team collaboration tools, making it a popular choice for UI design.

Adobe XD: Adobe XD is a vector-based design tool that allows designers to create interactive prototypes and animations for user interfaces. It offers a range of features, such as responsive design, design systems, and team collaboration tools, making it a comprehensive tool for UI design.

Testing and Refining Your User Interface Design Testing and refining your user interface design is an essential step in the design process. It can help you identify usability issues, improve the overall user experience, and ensure that your tool meets the needs of your target audience.

Conduct user testing: Conduct user testing to gather feedback from real users about your interface. This can include conducting surveys, usability testing, or focus groups to gather data on how users interact with your tool.

Refine your design: Use the feedback gathered from user testing to refine your design and improve the overall user experience. This can include making changes to the layout, navigation, or interactive elements to make your tool more user-friendly.

Continuously test and iterate: Continuously test and iterate your design throughout the development process to ensure that your tool meets the needs of your users. This can include conducting additional user testing, making design changes, and incorporating feedback from your users.

Chapter 5: Building the Backend

The backend of a chatbot or art generator is the foundation of the tool, as it is responsible for generating responses or creating digital art based on user input. In this chapter, we will explore the technical details of building the backend of your tool, including how to structure your code, how to incorporate APIs and libraries, and how to handle user input and output.

Structuring Your Code

The structure of your code is critical to the functionality and scalability of your chatbot or art generator. When building the backend of your tool, you should aim to follow best practices in coding, such as using modular design principles, commenting your code, and adhering to coding standards.

Modular design principles involve breaking down your code into smaller, more manageable modules that can be tested and developed separately. This approach enables you to reuse code across different parts of your project and makes it easier to maintain your code in the long term.

Commenting your code is also essential for maintaining your codebase, as it provides context and explanations for different sections of your code. It can also help other developers understand your code more easily and make it easier to debug errors.

Finally, adhering to coding standards can ensure that your code is consistent, readable, and maintainable. Standards such as PEP8 for Python and ESLint for JavaScript can help you ensure that your code is consistent and readable.

Incorporating APIs and Libraries

Incorporating APIs and libraries is a crucial part of building the backend of your chatbot or art generator. APIs allow your code to interact with external services, such as natural language processing tools or art generation libraries. Libraries are collections of pre-written code that you can incorporate into your project to save time and effort.

When incorporating APIs and libraries, you should consider factors such as performance, reliability, and ease of use. You should also ensure that the APIs and libraries you choose are compatible with your programming language and the other tools you are using in your project.

Handling User Input and Output

Handling user input and output is an essential part of building the backend of your chatbot or art generator. When designing the backend, you should consider how users will interact with your tool and how you will handle their input.

For chatbots, you will need to develop code that can interpret and respond to user input. This can involve using natural language processing tools to understand the user's intent and generate appropriate responses. You will also need to consider how you will handle different types of input, such as text, voice, or images.

For art generators, you will need to develop code that can interpret user input and generate unique pieces of digital art based on that input. This can involve using machine learning or neural networks to generate art based on input data such as images or text.

Optimizing Your Code

Optimizing your code is an essential part of building the backend of your chatbot or art generator. Optimizing your code can help you improve performance and scalability, reduce load times, and minimize memory usage.

There are several techniques you can use to optimize your code, such as caching frequently used data, minimizing database queries, and using efficient algorithms. You should also consider using profiling tools to identify performance bottlenecks in your code and improve overall performance.

Testing and Debugging Your Code

Testing and debugging your code are critical to ensuring that your chatbot or art generator is functioning correctly. Testing involves running your code through a series of tests to ensure that it is generating the expected output. Debugging involves identifying and fixing errors or bugs in your code.

There are several types of testing you can use to test your code, such as unit testing, integration testing, and end-to-end testing. You should also consider using automated testing tools to speed up the process.

Scaling and Optimization

Once you have a working backend, it's important to consider how your system will scale as more users begin to use your chatbot or art generator. As the number of users increases, the demands on your system will grow, and it will become necessary to optimize your code to ensure that it can handle the increased load.

One approach to optimizing your code is to use caching. Caching is the process of storing frequently accessed data in a cache, which can then be quickly retrieved when needed. By using caching, you can reduce the number of requests to external APIs or databases, which can improve the performance of your system.

Another approach to optimizing your code is to use load balancing. Load balancing is the process of distributing incoming traffic across multiple servers to ensure that no single server becomes overwhelmed. By using load balancing, you can improve the reliability and performance of your system, even as the number of users grows.

Testing and Debugging

Testing and debugging are critical components of building any software system, and chatbots and art generators are no exception. To ensure that your system is functioning correctly, you will need to develop a testing and debugging strategy that covers all aspects of your system, from the user interface to the backend code.

One approach to testing and debugging is to use automated testing tools. Automated testing tools can help you quickly and efficiently test your system and can even identify potential issues before they become problems. Some popular automated testing tools for chatbots and art generators include Botium, TestMyBot, and Chatbase.

Another approach to testing and debugging is to use manual testing. Manual testing involves manually testing your system, either by interacting with your chatbot or by creating test cases for your art generator. Manual testing can be time-consuming, but it can also help you identify potential issues that automated testing tools might miss.

Finally, it's important to have a plan in place for debugging any issues that arise. When a user reports a problem with your chatbot or art generator, you will need to be able to quickly identify the root cause of the issue and develop a fix. Having a well-defined debugging process in place can help you quickly resolve issues and ensure that your system remains functional and reliable.

Building a chatbot or art generator can be a complex and challenging process, but by following the steps outlined in this chapter, you can develop a powerful and effective tool that meets the needs of your users. Whether you are building a chatbot to improve customer service or an art generator to create unique pieces of digital art, the principles of backend development remain the same. By focusing on modularity, scalability, and testing and debugging, you can develop a tool that is reliable, efficient, and effective.

Chapter 6: Incorporating Machine Learning and NLP

Machine learning and natural language processing (NLP) are two of the most exciting and rapidly evolving fields in computer science, with countless applications in areas ranging from healthcare to finance to entertainment. In the realm of chatbot and art generator development, these technologies can be used to create more sophisticated and personalized user experiences, with chatbots that can understand and respond to natural language queries, and art generators that can learn and adapt to user preferences.

In this chapter, we will explore the technical details of incorporating machine learning and NLP into your chatbot or art generator. We will cover the basics of machine learning and NLP, including the different types of machine learning models and NLP algorithms, and how to train and evaluate these models using popular tools like TensorFlow and Keras. Additionally, we will discuss the best practices for incorporating machine learning and NLP into your chatbot or art generator, including managing user data and ensuring privacy and security.

Understanding Machine Learning:

Machine learning is a type of artificial intelligence that enables computers to learn from data and make predictions or decisions without being explicitly programmed to do so. There are several different types of machine learning models, including supervised learning, unsupervised learning, and reinforcement learning.

Supervised learning involves training a model on a labeled dataset, where each example in the dataset is associated with a known output or label. The goal of supervised learning is to learn a function that can map inputs to outputs, based on the patterns in the labeled data. Examples of supervised learning applications in chatbots might include training a model to recognize the intent behind user queries, or to generate appropriate responses to specific types of questions.

Unsupervised learning, on the other hand, involves training a model on an unlabeled dataset, where there is no predefined output or label. The goal of unsupervised learning is to discover patterns or structure in the data, without any specific task in mind. Examples of unsupervised learning applications in art generators might include training a model to generate abstract patterns or to cluster similar images together based on their visual features.

Reinforcement learning involves training a model to make decisions based on feedback from the environment, such as rewards or penalties. The goal of reinforcement learning is to learn an optimal policy for taking actions in a given environment, based on the feedback from that environment. Examples of reinforcement learning applications in chatbots might include training a model to recommend products or services based on user preferences, or to provide personalized responses based on user feedback.

Training Machine Learning Models:

To train a machine learning model, you need a dataset of input-output pairs, along with a way to evaluate the performance of the model on new, unseen examples. The process of training a machine learning model typically involves several steps, including data preprocessing, model selection, hyperparameter tuning, and evaluation.

Data preprocessing involves cleaning and formatting the input data to make it suitable for training a machine learning model. This might involve tasks like tokenization, stemming, and lemmatization for text data, or image normalization and resizing for image data.

Model selection involves choosing the type of machine learning model to use for a given task, as well as the architecture and parameters of that model. This might involve tasks like selecting a neural network architecture for image classification or choosing a decision tree algorithm for classification of categorical data.

Hyperparameter tuning involves adjusting the parameters of the machine learning model to optimize its performance on the validation set. This might involve tasks like adjusting the learning rate of a neural network or the regularization parameter of a support vector machine.

Evaluation involves testing the performance of the trained model on a separate test dataset, to ensure that it is able to generalize to new, unseen examples. This might involve metrics like accuracy, precision, recall, or F1 score, depending on the specific

Neural Language Generation:

Another approach to NLP is neural language generation, which is a subfield of deep learning that involves training neural networks to generate text. Neural language generation is an effective approach for creating natural-sounding chatbot responses, as it allows the chatbot to learn from a large corpus of text data and generate responses that mimic human language patterns.

The most common type of neural language generation model is the recurrent neural network (RNN), which is designed to handle sequential data like text. RNNs work by processing each word in a sentence one at a time and maintaining a hidden state that captures information about the words that came before it. The hidden state is then used to generate the next word in the sentence, and the process is repeated until the entire sentence is generated.

One of the main challenges of using neural language generation in chatbots is the risk of generating inappropriate or offensive responses. Neural language generation models are highly dependent on the data they are trained on, and if the training data includes biased or inappropriate language, the model may generate similar responses. Therefore, it is important to carefully curate the training data and regularly monitor the chatbot's responses to ensure that they are appropriate and respectful.

Best Practices for Incorporating Machine Learning and NLP

Incorporating machine learning and NLP into your chatbot can be a powerful way to create a more effective and natural-sounding tool. However, there are several best practices to keep in mind when working with these technologies to ensure that your chatbot is accurate, reliable, and respectful.

Curate your training data carefully: The accuracy of your machine learning and NLP models is highly dependent on the quality of the training data. Therefore, it is important to carefully select and curate your training data to ensure that it is representative of the language and patterns that your chatbot will encounter in the real world.

Regularly monitor your chatbot's responses: Even with careful training data curation, there is always a risk that your chatbot will generate inappropriate or offensive responses. Therefore, it is important to regularly monitor your chatbot's responses and intervene if necessary to ensure that they are appropriate and respectful.

Use appropriate evaluation metrics: When evaluating the performance of your machine learning and NLP models, it is important to use appropriate metrics that take into account the nuances of language and user interactions. For example, accuracy metrics may not be appropriate for evaluating chatbot performance, as users may have different ways of phrasing their questions or may not use proper spelling or grammar.

Consider the ethical implications of your chatbot: As with any technology, chatbots can have ethical implications, particularly when it comes to issues of privacy and bias. It is important to consider these implications when designing and building your chatbot, and to take steps to ensure that your chatbot is respectful of user privacy and does not perpetuate bias or discrimination.

Incorporating machine learning and NLP into your chatbot can be a powerful way to create a more effective and natural-sounding tool. However, it is important to understand the technical details of these technologies and to follow best practices to ensure that your chatbot is accurate, reliable, and respectful. With careful planning and implementation, machine learning and NLP can take your chatbot to the next level, providing users with a seamless and enjoyable experience.

Chapter 7: Optimizing for Performance and Scalability

Once your chatbot or art generator is up and running, it is important to optimize its performance and scalability to ensure that it can handle high levels of traffic and operate efficiently. This chapter will cover the technical details of optimizing your tool for performance and scalability, including how to implement caching, how to use load balancing, and how to manage resources effectively.

Section 1: Understanding Performance and Scalability- In this section, we will explore the concepts of performance and scalability and how they relate to chatbot and art generator development. We will discuss the importance of performance and scalability, and why it is essential to optimize your tool to ensure it can handle high levels of traffic and operate efficiently.

Understanding Performance and Scalability in Chatbot and Art Generator Development

Performance and scalability are critical aspects of building effective chatbots and art generators. These two concepts are closely related and play a vital role in determining the success and usability of these tools. In this section, we will delve into the concepts of performance and scalability and explore their importance in the context of chatbot and art generator development. We will also discuss why optimizing these tools for performance and scalability is essential to ensure they can handle high levels of traffic and operate efficiently.

Performance in Chatbot and Art Generator Development

Performance refers to the speed and efficiency with which a chatbot or art generator responds to user input or generates art. It is an essential aspect of user experience, as slow response times or delays can frustrate users and lead to poor user satisfaction. High-performance chatbots and art generators are crucial in providing a seamless and enjoyable experience for users, as they can quickly generate responses or art and provide real-time interactions.

Several factors affect the performance of chatbots and art generators. One of the key factors is the underlying technology or platform used to build the chatbot or art generator. Different technologies, such as rule-based systems, natural language processing (NLP), machine learning (ML), or deep learning, have different performance characteristics. For instance, rule-based systems tend to be faster in responding to user input as they rely on predefined rules and do not require complex processing. On the other hand, ML or deep learning-based chatbots and art generators may require more processing time as they rely on training data and complex algorithms.

Another factor that impacts performance is the complexity of the chatbot or art generator's logic or algorithms. The more complex the logic or algorithms, the more processing power and time it may require to generate responses or art. Therefore, optimizing the logic or algorithms used in chatbots and art generators is crucial for achieving high performance.

Moreover, the quality and efficiency of the code used to build the chatbot or art generator also significantly impact performance. Well-optimized code that is free from unnecessary redundancies or inefficient operations can lead to faster response times and smoother interactions. Therefore, optimizing the codebase of a chatbot or art generator is an essential aspect of improving its performance.

Scalability in Chatbot and Art Generator Development

Scalability refers to the ability of a chatbot or art generator to handle increasing levels of traffic or workload without a significant drop in performance or user experience. It is a critical aspect of building robust and reliable chatbots and art generators that can handle high levels of demand and grow as the user base expands.

Scalability is crucial in chatbot and art generator development because these tools are often expected to handle a large number of simultaneous users or requests. For instance, in the case of a customer support chatbot, it may need to handle multiple user inquiries simultaneously, especially during peak hours. Similarly, an art generator may receive numerous requests from users to generate art in real-time. Therefore, it is essential to ensure that chatbots and art generators can handle such high levels of traffic without compromising on performance.

Several factors affect the scalability of chatbots and art generators. One of the key factors is the architecture used to build these tools. The architecture should be designed in such a way that it can scale horizontally, meaning it can handle increased traffic by adding more resources, such as servers or instances, to the system. A well-designed architecture should also be able to distribute the workload efficiently across multiple resources to prevent any single point of failure.

Another factor that impacts scalability is the efficiency of the data storage and retrieval mechanisms used in chatbots and art generators. As these tools often rely on databases or other data storage mechanisms to store and retrieve user data or generated art, optimizing these mechanisms for high performance and scalability is crucial. Techniques such as data caching, indexing, and database sharding can be employed to improve the efficiency and scalability of data storage and retrieval.

Additionally, the way chatbots and art generators handle user sessions and state management can also affect scalability. Session management refers to how the tool keeps track of user interactions and maintains the context of the conversation. Efficient session management can prevent unnecessary overhead and improve the scalability of the tool.

Techniques such as session tokenization, stateless design, or distributed session management can be employed to optimize session handling in chatbots and art generators.

Importance of Performance and Scalability in Chatbot and Art Generator Development

The importance of performance and scalability cannot be overstated in the development of chatbots and art generators. These two aspects directly impact the user experience and usability of the tools and determine their effectiveness in fulfilling their intended purpose.

Firstly, performance is crucial in ensuring that chatbots and art generators can generate responses or art in real-time or with minimal delays. Users expect quick and efficient interactions with these tools, and any performance bottlenecks can lead to frustration and dissatisfaction. High-performance chatbots and art generators can provide smooth and seamless interactions, which can lead to higher user satisfaction, engagement, and retention. On the other hand, poor performance can result in users abandoning the tool and seeking alternatives.

Secondly, scalability is vital in ensuring that chatbots and art generators can handle increased traffic or workload as the user base grows. These tools are often expected to handle multiple requests simultaneously and provide uninterrupted service even during peak hours. Scalability ensures that the tool can accommodate the growing demand without suffering from performance degradation or downtime. It also allows for future growth and expansion of the user base without needing significant changes to the tool's architecture or infrastructure.

Optimizing for Performance and Scalability in Chatbot and Art Generator Development

Optimizing for performance and scalability requires careful consideration of various aspects of chatbot and art generator development. Here are some key areas that can be optimized to achieve high performance and scalability:

Algorithm and Logic Optimization: The algorithms and logic used in chatbots and art generators can be optimized to improve performance. This can include optimizing the NLP or ML algorithms used for understanding user input, generating responses or art, and managing conversations. Techniques such as algorithmic complexity analysis, code profiling, and performance testing can be employed to identify and address any performance bottlenecks in the algorithms or logic.

Codebase Optimization: The codebase of the chatbot or art generator can be optimized to improve performance and scalability. This can include removing redundant code, optimizing data structures and algorithms, and minimizing unnecessary computations. Clean and efficient code can lead to faster response times and smoother interactions, thereby improving performance. Additionally, employing best practices for coding standards, error handling, and resource management can also contribute to better performance and scalability.

Data Storage and Retrieval Optimization: Efficiently storing and retrieving data is crucial for performance and scalability in chatbots and art generators. Techniques such as data caching, indexing, and database sharding can be employed to optimize data storage and retrieval. Caching frequently used data, indexing data for quick retrieval, and distributing data across multiple resources can improve the efficiency of data operations, leading to better performance and scalability.

Session and State Management Optimization: Efficiently managing user sessions and state information is critical for chatbots and art generators. Techniques such as tokenization, stateless design, or distributed session management can be employed to optimize session and state management. This can prevent unnecessary overhead and reduce the storage and processing requirements, leading to improved performance and scalability.

Architecture and Infrastructure Optimization: The architecture and infrastructure used to build the chatbot or art generator can be optimized for scalability. Employing a horizontally scalable architecture that can handle increased traffic by adding more resources can improve scalability.

Using cloud-based infrastructure that can dynamically scale up or down based on demand can also enhance scalability. Additionally, employing techniques such as load balancing, auto-scaling, and caching at different layers of the application stack can improve performance and scalability.

Response Time Optimization: The response time of a chatbot or art generator is crucial for providing a seamless user experience. Techniques such as asynchronous processing, parallel processing, and optimized API calls can be employed to reduce response times. Minimizing processing delays, network latency, and computational overhead can contribute to faster response times, thereby improving performance.

Error Handling and Fault Tolerance: Proper error handling and fault tolerance mechanisms can improve the performance and scalability of chatbots and art generators. Implementing error detection, handling, and recovery mechanisms can prevent the system from crashing or slowing down due to errors or failures. Techniques such as retrying failed requests, handling timeouts, and graceful degradation can help maintain the performance and availability of the tool, even in the presence of errors or failures.

Testing and Performance Monitoring: Continuous testing and performance monitoring are essential for identifying and addressing performance and scalability issues. Techniques such as load testing, stress testing, and performance profiling can be employed to assess the performance of the chatbot or art generator under different conditions. Monitoring key performance metrics such as response time, resource utilization, and error rates can help identify performance bottlenecks and optimize the tool accordingly.

User Experience Optimization: The user experience plays a significant role in the performance and scalability of chatbots and art generators. An intuitive and user-friendly interface can reduce the learning curve and enable users to interact more efficiently with the tool. Techniques such as contextual guidance, error handling, and feedback mechanisms can enhance the user experience and contribute to better performance and scalability.

Continuous Optimization: Performance and scalability optimization is an ongoing process that requires continuous monitoring and improvement. As the user base grows, the workload increases, and new features are added, the chatbot or art generator may require further optimization. Regularly analyzing performance metrics, user feedback, and system logs can help identify areas that need optimization and ensure that the tool continues to perform efficiently and scale effectively.

Understanding and optimizing for performance and scalability are critical aspects of developing a chatbot or art generator. High performance and scalability are essential for providing a seamless user experience, handling high levels of traffic, and ensuring the efficient operation of the tool. Optimizing various aspects such as algorithms, codebase, data storage and retrieval, session management, architecture, response time, error handling, user experience, and continuous monitoring is necessary to achieve optimal performance and scalability.

By carefully considering and implementing performance and scalability optimization techniques, developers can create chatbots and art generators that can handle increased workload, provide fast and efficient responses, and deliver a satisfying user experience. Regular monitoring and continuous optimization are essential to ensure that the tool remains performant and scalable as the user base grows and evolves. A well-optimized chatbot or art generator has the potential to drive user engagement, satisfaction, and retention, and ultimately contribute to the success of the overall application or service.

Section 2: Techniques for Optimizing Performance

Performance optimization is a critical aspect of developing chatbots and art generators to ensure that they deliver fast and efficient responses, provide a seamless user experience, and operate efficiently even under high levels of traffic. In this section, we will explore various techniques that readers can use to optimize the performance of their chatbot or art generator. We will discuss topics such as caching, code optimization, and database optimization, and provide guidance on how to implement these techniques effectively.

Caching-

Caching is a technique used to store frequently used data or computations in a temporary storage location so that they can be quickly retrieved without being recalculated or fetched from the original data source. Caching can significantly improve the performance of chatbots and art generators by reducing the need to repeat resource-intensive operations.

There are different types of caching that can be implemented to optimize performance:

a. Data Caching: Data caching involves storing frequently accessed data in a cache to reduce the need to fetch the same data from the original data source multiple times. For example, if a chatbot retrieves data from an external API, the response can be cached so that subsequent requests for the same data can be quickly retrieved from the cache instead of making additional API calls.

b. Result Caching: Result caching involves storing the results of resource-intensive operations in a cache to avoid repeating the same operation multiple times. For example, if an art generator applies a complex image processing algorithm to generate an image, the result of the algorithm can be cached so that it can be quickly retrieved for subsequent requests without reapplying the same algorithm.

c. Full-page Caching: Full-page caching involves storing entire web pages or responses in a cache to serve them directly from the cache instead of dynamically generating the response for each request. This can be particularly useful for chatbots or art generators that generate static or relatively static content, as it can significantly reduce the server-side processing overhead and improve response times.

When implementing caching, it's important to carefully consider what data or computations should be cached, how long the cache should be retained, and how the cache should be invalidated or updated when the underlying data changes. Caching strategies can vary depending on the specific requirements of the chatbot or art generator and the type of data or computations being cached. Implementing an efficient caching mechanism requires thorough planning, monitoring, and tuning to ensure that the cache is effectively utilized and does not introduce stale or outdated data.

Code Optimization-

Code optimization involves making improvements to the code of a chatbot or art generator to make it more efficient and performant. Optimizing the code can help reduce processing overhead, minimize resource utilization, and improve response times.

There are several techniques that can be employed for code optimization:

a. Algorithm Optimization: Optimizing the algorithms used in chatbots and art generators can have a significant impact on performance. Analyzing and improving the efficiency of algorithms can help reduce processing time and improve the overall performance of the tool. Techniques such as algorithmic complexity analysis, algorithmic design patterns, and algorithmic optimization can be employed to optimize the algorithms used in the tool.

b. Code Refactoring: Refactoring involves restructuring the code to improve its readability, maintainability, and performance. By eliminating redundant code, optimizing loops, improving data structures, and reducing code complexity, code refactoring can help improve the efficiency of the chatbot or art generator. Applying best practices such as modularization, abstraction, and encapsulation can also contribute to code optimization.

c. Resource Utilization Optimization: Optimizing resource utilization involves efficiently managing system resources such as CPU, memory, and disk I/O to minimize resource contention and maximize performance. Techniques such as resource profiling, resource monitoring, and resource tuning can be employed to identify and address resource utilization bottlene lenecks in the chatbot or art generator. For example, optimizing memory usage by reducing unnecessary object creation, minimizing I/O operations, and optimizing database queries can significantly improve performance.

d. Parallelism and Concurrency: Parallelism and concurrency involve leveraging the capabilities of modern hardware, such as multi-core processors, to perform tasks in parallel or concurrently, thereby improving performance. Techniques such as multi-threading, asynchronous programming, and parallel processing can be employed to optimize the processing of tasks in the chatbot or art generator. However, it's important to carefully manage parallelism and concurrency to avoid issues such as race conditions and deadlocks, which can degrade performance or cause unintended behavior.

Database Optimization-

The database plays a crucial role in the performance of chatbots and art generators that rely on persistent data storage. Database optimization involves improving the efficiency of database operations to minimize query times, reduce resource utilization, and improve overall system performance.

There are several techniques that can be employed for database optimization:

a. Indexing: Indexing involves creating indexes on database columns to improve the speed of data retrieval operations. Indexes allow the database to quickly locate and retrieve data based on the indexed columns, which can significantly reduce query times. Carefully choosing which columns to index, and avoiding unnecessary or redundant indexes, can greatly improve database performance.

b. Query Optimization: Query optimization involves optimizing the SQL queries used to retrieve or manipulate data in the database. Techniques such as analyzing query execution plans, using appropriate join types, minimizing subqueries, and avoiding unnecessary or inefficient queries can greatly improve database performance. Using prepared statements or parameterized queries can also help prevent SQL injection attacks and improve query performance.

c. Database Denormalization: Denormalization involves structuring the database to reduce the number of joins required to retrieve data, thereby improving query performance. By storing redundant data or pre-calculating aggregations, denormalization can reduce the processing overhead of the database and improve overall system performance. However, denormalization should be carefully considered, as it can introduce data redundancy and maintenance complexity.

d. Caching: Caching, as discussed earlier, can also be applied to databases to store frequently accessed data or query results in a cache, reducing the need to fetch the same data from the database multiple times. This can greatly improve the performance of database-intensive operations in chatbots and art generators.

Performance Monitoring and Testing-

Performance monitoring and testing are essential for optimizing the performance of chatbots and art generators. Monitoring involves measuring and analyzing various performance metrics during runtime to identify performance bottlenecks and areas for improvement. Testing involves running performance tests to simulate high levels of traffic and measure the response times, resource utilization, and overall system performance.

a. Performance Monitoring: Performance monitoring involves using monitoring tools, logging, and profiling techniques to measure and analyze various performance metrics, such as response times, CPU utilization, memory usage, and database query times. This can help identify performance bottlenecks, resource contention, or inefficient code or database operations that need optimization. Real-time monitoring can provide insights into the system behavior during runtime and help in making informed decisions for performance optimization.

b. Performance Testing: Performance testing involves running performance tests to simulate high levels of traffic and measure the response times, resource utilization, and overall system performance. Performance testing can help identify the system's capacity, scalability, and response times under different levels of load. Techniques such as load testing, stress testing, and scalability testing can be employed to measure the performance of the chatbot or art generator and identify areas for improvement.

Scalability Techniques-

Scalability is an important aspect of performance optimization as it determines the system's ability to handle increasing levels of traffic without degrading performance. Implementing scalability techniques can ensure that chatbots and art generators can handle high levels of traffic and user interactions without experiencing performance degradation.

There are several scalability techniques that can be employed:

a. Horizontal Scaling: Horizontal scaling involves adding more resources, such as servers or instances, to the system to handle increased traffic and user load. This can be achieved by distributing the workload across multiple servers, which can improve system performance and response times. Techniques such as load balancing, clustering, and sharding can be employed to achieve horizontal scalability in chatbots and art generators.

b. Vertical Scaling: Vertical scaling involves upgrading the system resources, such as increasing CPU, memory, or storage capacity, of a single server to handle increased load. This can be achieved by upgrading the server hardware or optimizing the server configurations to improve performance. Vertical scaling can be a cost-effective approach for small-scale chatbots or art generators that may not require a large number of servers.

c. Cloud-based Scaling: Cloud-based scaling involves leveraging cloud computing platforms and services to dynamically allocate resources based on the system's demand. Cloud-based platforms, such as Amazon Web Services (AWS), Microsoft Azure, and Google Cloud, provide auto-scaling capabilities that automatically adjust the resources based on system load. This can ensure optimal performance during peak loads and reduce costs during low loads.

d. Microservices Architecture: Microservices architecture involves breaking down the system into smaller, loosely coupled, and independently deployable services. Each service can be scaled independently based on its load and performance requirements. Microservices architecture can enable better scalability, as it allows for flexibility in adding or removing services based on demand, and can prevent the performance degradation of the entire system due to a single service's performance issues.

Continuous Performance Optimization-

Performance optimization is an ongoing process, and continuous monitoring and improvement are required to ensure optimal performance of chatbots and art generators. Regularly reviewing and analyzing performance metrics, identifying and addressing performance bottlenecks, and optimizing code and database operations can help maintain optimal performance over time.

a. Performance Profiling: Performance profiling involves using profiling tools or techniques to identify performance bottlenecks in the system. Profiling can provide insights into the areas of the system that consume excessive resources, have long execution times, or suffer from inefficient operations. Profiling can help identify the specific areas of the code or database operations that need optimization.

b. Code Review and Refactoring: Regular code review and refactoring can help identify and fix performance issues in the codebase. Code review involves reviewing the code for best practices, optimization opportunities, and potential performance issues. Refactoring involves restructuring the code to optimize resource usage, reduce redundancy, and improve overall system performance. Regular code review and refactoring can help maintain clean and efficient code, and prevent performance degradation over time.

c. Performance Testing: Regular performance testing can help identify performance degradation or regressions in the system. Performance tests should be run periodically, especially after implementing changes or optimizations, to ensure that the system's performance is maintained or improved. Performance testing can also help identify any new performance bottlenecks that may have emerged due to changes in the system or increased load.

d. Stay Updated with Latest Technologies and Best Practices: Technology and best practices in software development and performance optimization are constantly evolving. It's important to stay updated with the latest technologies, tools, and best practices to ensure optimal performance of chatbots and art generators. Regularly reviewing industry standards, guidelines, and performance optimization techniques can help identify new opportunities for improving system performance.

Optimizing performance is a crucial aspect of developing chatbots and art generators that deliver a seamless and satisfying user experience. Techniques such as caching, code optimization, database optimization, parallelism and concurrency, scalability, and continuous performance optimization can significantly improve the performance of chatbots and art generators. By carefully analyzing performance metrics, identifying performance bottlenecks, and implementing appropriate optimizations.

Section 3: Techniques for Improving Scalability

In this section, we will delve into various techniques that can be employed to improve the scalability of chatbots and art generators. Scalability is the ability of a system to handle increasing loads of traffic, users, and data without experiencing performance degradation or downtime. As the demand for chatbots and art generators grows, it is essential to ensure that these systems can handle increasing loads efficiently. Here, we will discuss key techniques such as load balancing, vertical and horizontal scaling, and auto-scaling, and provide guidance on how to effectively implement these techniques.

Load Balancing-

Load balancing is a technique used to distribute incoming requests or workload evenly across multiple servers to optimize resource utilization and prevent overloading of any single server. By distributing the load, load balancing ensures that no single server is overwhelmed, which helps improve system performance, response times, and availability.

There are several load balancing techniques that can be implemented in chatbots and art generators:

a. Round Robin Load Balancing: In this technique, incoming requests are evenly distributed across multiple servers in a sequential manner. Each server in the rotation receives an equal share of requests, and the load is balanced based on the order of the servers in the rotation. Round Robin load balancing is simple to implement and does not require complex algorithms or monitoring, making it a cost-effective option for small-scale systems.

b. Weighted Round Robin Load Balancing: This technique is similar to Round Robin load balancing, but it allows for assigning different weights to each server in the rotation based on its capacity or capability. Servers with higher capacities can be assigned higher weights, which means they will receive a larger share of requests compared to servers with lower weights. Weighted Round Robin load balancing can be used to achieve better resource utilization and performance optimization in systems with servers of varying capacities.

c. Least Connection Load Balancing: In this technique, incoming requests are distributed to servers based on the number of active connections on each server. Servers with fewer active connections receive more requests, while servers with more active connections receive fewer requests. This ensures that requests are evenly distributed based on the actual workload of each server, which can help prevent overloading of servers with heavy traffic.

d. Dynamic Load Balancing: Dynamic load balancing involves continuously monitoring the performance and resource utilization of servers and adjusting the load distribution based on real-time data. Servers that are performing well and have lower resource utilization receive more requests, while servers that are struggling with high resource utilization receive fewer requests. Dynamic load balancing allows for optimal resource allocation based on the actual performance of servers, which can help improve system performance and response times.

Vertical and Horizontal Scaling-

Vertical and horizontal scaling are techniques used to increase the capacity and capability of a system to handle increased loads. Vertical scaling involves upgrading the resources of a single server, such as increasing CPU, memory, or storage capacity, to handle increased load. This can be achieved by upgrading the server hardware, optimizing the server configurations, or using more powerful servers. Vertical scaling can be a cost-effective approach for small-scale chatbots or art generators that may not require a large number of servers.

On the other hand, horizontal scaling involves adding more resources, such as servers or instances, to the system to handle increased traffic and user load. This can be achieved by distributing the workload across multiple servers, which can improve system performance and response times. Techniques such as load balancing, clustering, and sharding can be employed to achieve horizontal scalability in chatbots and art generators. Horizontal scaling allows for better scalability as it allows for adding more servers as needed to handle increased loads, and can be more cost-effective in handling large-scale systems.

Auto-Scaling-

Auto-scaling is a technique that involves automatically adjusting the resources of a system based on its demand. Auto-scaling allows for dynamically adding or removing servers or instances based on the current workload, without manual intervention. This ensures that the system can handle varying loads efficiently, without overloading or underutilizing resources.

There are several auto-scaling techniques that can be implemented in chatbots and art generators:

a. Reactive Auto-Scaling: In this approach, auto-scaling is triggered reactively based on predefined thresholds, such as CPU utilization, memory usage, or request rate. When the workload exceeds a certain threshold, new servers or instances are automatically added to the system to handle the increased load. Conversely, when the workload decreases, servers or instances are automatically removed to save costs and resources. Reactive auto-scaling is a simple approach that can be effective in handling predictable workload patterns.

b. Proactive Auto-Scaling: Proactive auto-scaling involves analyzing historical data and predicting future workload patterns to proactively adjust the resources of the system. Machine learning algorithms can be used to analyze data, identify patterns, and make predictions about future workloads. Based on these predictions, the system can automatically add or remove servers or instances to handle anticipated load changes. Proactive auto-scaling can help optimize resource allocation and ensure that the system is prepared to handle changing workload patterns.

c. Hybrid Auto-Scaling: Hybrid auto-scaling combines both reactive and proactive approaches to optimize resource allocation. It involves setting up predefined thresholds for reactive auto-scaling and using machine learning algorithms for proactive auto-scaling. This allows for dynamically adjusting resources based on real-time workload changes as well as predicted workload patterns, providing a balanced and efficient approach to auto-scaling.

Database Optimization-

The database is a critical component of chatbots and art generators, as it stores and retrieves data required for generating responses, maintaining conversations, and managing user interactions. Database optimization is essential to ensure that the database can handle increased loads and provide fast and efficient data retrieval and storage.

There are several techniques for optimizing the database in chatbots and art generators:

a. Indexing: Indexing involves creating indexes on the database tables to optimize data retrieval. Indexes are data structures that allow for fast and efficient data retrieval based on specific columns or fields. By creating indexes on frequently used columns or fields, the database can retrieve data quickly without performing full table scans, which can significantly improve query performance.

b. Denormalization: Denormalization involves reducing the number of joins or relationships between tables in the database to improve query performance. By storing redundant data or duplicating data across tables, denormalization can eliminate the need for complex joins, which can be time-consuming and resource-intensive. However, denormalization should be used judiciously to avoid data inconsistency and redundancy.

c. Caching: Caching involves storing frequently accessed data in memory or in a separate caching layer to improve data retrieval performance. Caching can be used to store frequently accessed data, such as user profiles, conversation history, or frequently used responses, to reduce the load on the database and provide faster data retrieval. Caching can be implemented using technologies such as in-memory databases, distributed caching, or content delivery networks (CDNs), depending on the system requirements and architecture.

d. Database Partitioning: Database partitioning involves dividing a large database into smaller partitions based on certain criteria, such as time, region, or user. Each partition is stored separately and can be accessed independently, which can improve query performance and data retrieval. Database partitioning can be implemented using techniques such as horizontal partitioning, vertical partitioning, or hybrid partitioning, depending on the system requirements and data access patterns.

Code Optimization-

Code optimization involves optimizing the code of the chatbot or art generator to improve performance and resource utilization. Efficient and optimized code can help reduce response times, CPU usage, and memory usage, resulting in a more responsive and efficient system. Here are some techniques for code optimization in chatbots and art generators:

a. Algorithmic Optimization: Algorithmic optimization involves optimizing the algorithms and logic used in the chatbot or art generator. This includes identifying and removing redundant or unnecessary calculations, simplifying complex algorithms, and optimizing data structures and algorithms for better performance. Algorithmic optimization can significantly improve the efficiency of the system and reduce the processing overhead.

b. Memory Management: Efficient memory management is crucial for optimizing performance in chatbots and art generators. This includes minimizing memory usage by reducing unnecessary data storage, deallocating memory when it is no longer needed, and optimizing data structures to minimize memory overhead. Proper memory management can help prevent memory leaks, reduce CPU usage, and improve overall system performance.

c. Code Profiling and Analysis: Code profiling and analysis involves using tools and techniques to analyze the performance and resource utilization of the code. Profiling can help identify performance bottlenecks, inefficient code, and areas that require optimization. By analyzing the code, developers can make informed decisions on optimizing critical sections of the code, improving performance, and reducing resource utilization.

d. Code Refactoring: Code refactoring involves restructuring and optimizing the code without changing its functionality. This can include removing redundant code, simplifying complex code, and optimizing code for better performance. Code refactoring can help improve code readability, maintainability, and performance, resulting in a more efficient system.

e. Compilation and Optimization Flags: Compilers often provide optimization flags that can be used during the compilation process to optimize the generated code. These flags can include options to enable specific optimizations, such as loop unrolling, function inlining, and code size optimization. Using appropriate compilation and optimization flags can significantly improve the performance of the compiled code.

Load Balancing-

Load balancing is an essential technique for improving scalability in chatbots and art generators. Load balancing distributes the incoming workload evenly across multiple servers or instances to ensure that no single server or instance is overloaded, while others are underutilized. This helps prevent performance degradation, ensures high availability, and provides better overall system performance.

There are several load balancing techniques that can be implemented in chatbots and art generators:

a. Round Robin: In the round-robin load balancing technique, incoming requests are distributed evenly across multiple servers or instances in a cyclical manner. Each server or instance is assigned a request in a sequential order, and the process is repeated. Round-robin load balancing is simple to implement and can provide a basic level of load balancing. However, it may not be suitable for systems with varying workload patterns, as it does not take into account the actual load or capacity of each server or instance.

b. Least Connection: In the least connection load balancing technique, incoming requests are assigned to the server or instance with the fewest active connections. This helps distribute the workload based on the actual capacity and load of each server or instance, ensuring that heavily loaded servers or instances receive fewer requests, while underutilized servers or instances receive more requests. Least connection load balancing can help optimize resource utilization and improve system performance.

c. Session Affinity: Session affinity, also known as sticky session or session persistence, involves associating incoming requests from the same user or session with the same server or instance throughout the session duration. This ensures that all requests from the same user or session are directed to the same server or instance, maintaining the session state and providing consistent user experience. Session affinity can be implemented using techniques such as cookie-based affinity or source IP-based affinity.

d. Dynamic Load Balancing: Dynamic load balancing involves continuously monitoring the load and capacity of each server or instance and dynamically adjusting the load balancing algorithm based on the current workload. This can include reassigning requests to different servers or instances based on their current load, capacity, and performance metrics. Dynamic load balancing allows for better adaptability to changing workload patterns and ensures that the resources are efficiently utilized for optimal performance.

Vertical and Horizontal Scaling-

Vertical and horizontal scaling are techniques used to improve scalability in chatbots and art generators by adding more resources to the system.

a. Vertical Scaling: Vertical scaling, also known as scaling up, involves adding more resources to a single server or instance to handle increased workload. This can include upgrading the CPU, memory, storage, or other hardware components of the server or instance to increase its capacity. Vertical scaling can provide immediate performance improvements, as the server or instance has more resources to handle the workload. However, there are limitations to vertical scaling, as there is a limit to the capacity of a single server or instance.

b. Horizontal Scaling: Horizontal scaling, also known as scaling out, involves adding more servers or instances to the system to handle increased workload. This can be achieved by adding more physical servers or virtual machines to the system and distributing the workload across them. Horizontal scaling allows for virtually unlimited scalability, as more servers or instances can be added as needed to handle the workload. However, it requires proper load balancing and distributed system architecture to ensure that the workload is evenly distributed and resources are efficiently utilized.

Vertical and horizontal scaling can be used in combination to achieve optimal scalability in chatbots and art generators. Vertical scaling can be used for immediate performance improvements by adding more resources to the existing servers or instances, while horizontal scaling can be used for long-term scalability by adding more servers or instances to handle increased workload.

Auto-Scaling-

Auto-scaling is a technique that allows chatbots and art generators to automatically adjust the number of resources in the system based on the current workload. Auto-scaling ensures that the system can dynamically scale up or down based on the changing workload patterns, providing optimal performance while minimizing resource wastage.

Auto-scaling involves setting up rules or policies that define the conditions under which resources should be added or removed from the system. These conditions can be based on various metrics, such as CPU usage, memory usage, number of requests, or other performance metrics. When the conditions are met, auto-scaling mechanisms automatically add or remove resources from the system to maintain optimal performance.

There are several auto-scaling techniques that can be used in chatbots and art generators:

a. Reactive Auto-Scaling: Reactive auto-scaling involves adding or removing resources from the system in response to changes in workload patterns. For example, if the CPU usage exceeds a certain threshold, more resources can be added to the system to handle the increased workload. Similarly, if the CPU usage decreases, resources can be removed to avoid resource wastage. Reactive auto-scaling ensures that the system can adapt to changing workload patterns and provide optimal performance.

b. Proactive Auto-Scaling: Proactive auto-scaling involves predicting the future workload patterns based on historical data and adding or removing resources from the system in anticipation of the changes. For example, if the system experiences a surge in workload at a certain time of day based on historical data, proactive auto-scaling can add more resources to the system before the surge occurs, ensuring that the system can handle the workload without performance degradation. Proactive auto-scaling can help prevent performance issues before they occur and provide a more seamless user experience.

c. Event-Driven Auto-Scaling: Event-driven auto-scaling involves triggering auto-scaling actions based on specific events or conditions. For example, if a certain event occurs, such as a sudden spike in requests or an increase in error rates, auto-scaling can be triggered to add more resources to the system. Event-driven auto-scaling allows for quick and automatic response to changing conditions in the system, ensuring optimal performance.

Auto-scaling can be implemented using various tools and services provided by cloud providers, such as Amazon Web Services (AWS), Microsoft Azure, or Google Cloud Platform (GCP). These cloud-based services offer auto-scaling features that can be configured based on the specific requirements of the chatbot or art generator system.

Monitoring and Logging-

Monitoring and logging are critical techniques for improving the scalability of chatbots and art generators. Monitoring involves continuously observing and measuring various performance metrics of the system, such as CPU usage, memory usage, response times, error rates, and other relevant indicators. Logging involves recording important events and activities in the system, such as requests, responses, errors, and other relevant information.

Monitoring and logging allow for proactive identification and resolution of performance issues in real-time. By monitoring and logging the system, it is possible to detect performance bottlenecks, errors, and anomalies early on and take corrective actions to ensure optimal performance. Monitoring and logging also provide valuable insights into the system's behavior, resource utilization, and workload patterns, which can be used for capacity planning, performance tuning, and optimization.

There are various monitoring and logging tools available that can be integrated into chatbot or art generator systems. These tools can provide real-time monitoring and logging capabilities, as well as alerting and notification features to notify administrators or developers of any performance issues or anomalies in the system.

Performance Testing and Profiling-

Performance testing and profiling are techniques used to identify and address performance issues in chatbots and art generators. Performance testing involves systematically evaluating the system's performance under different workload scenarios, such as high load, low load, and peak load conditions. Performance testing can help identify performance bottlenecks, scalability limitations, and other issues that may affect the system's performance.

Profiling involves analyzing the system's code, configurations, and resources to identify areas that may impact performance. Profiling techniques, such as code profiling, memory profiling, and CPU profiling, can help identify inefficient code, resource-intensive operations, memory leaks, and other issues that may degrade the system's performance.

By conducting performance testing and profiling, it is possible to identify and address performance issues early in the development process. This can help optimize the system's performance, improve scalability, and ensure that the chatbot or art generator can handle the expected workload efficiently.

Continuous Monitoring and Optimization-

Scalability is an ongoing process that requires continuous monitoring and optimization. Once the chatbot or art generator is deployed, it is essential to continuously monitor the system's performance, workload patterns, and resource utilization to identify and address any performance issues or anomalies.

Continuous monitoring involves regularly reviewing performance metrics, logs, and other relevant data to detect any performance degradation, errors, or anomalies. It also involves setting up alerting and notification mechanisms to receive alerts or notifications when performance issues occur, so that prompt actions can be taken to address them.

Continuous optimization involves identifying and implementing optimizations to improve the system's performance and scalability. This can include code optimization, database optimization, caching, load balancing, auto-scaling adjustments, and other techniques discussed earlier. Continuous optimization ensures that the system is continually fine-tuned to achieve optimal performance and scalability based on the changing workload patterns and requirements.

Conclusion

In conclusion, optimizing the performance and scalability of chatbots and art generators is crucial for providing a seamless and responsive user experience. By implementing various techniques, such as caching, code optimization, database optimization, load balancing, vertical and horizontal scaling, auto-scaling, monitoring and logging, performance testing and profiling, and continuous monitoring and optimization, it is possible to ensure that the system can handle the expected workload efficiently and effectively.

It is important to carefully analyze the specific requirements and characteristics of the chatbot or art generator system and choose the appropriate techniques accordingly. Proper implementation of these techniques can help mitigate performance bottlene lenecks, improve resource utilization, reduce response times, minimize errors, and enhance scalability, resulting in a high-performing and scalable chatbot or art generator system.

When implementing these techniques, it is crucial to follow best practices and guidelines, test and validate the system's performance under different workload scenarios, and continuously monitor and optimize the system to ensure optimal performance. It is also essential to consider factors such as cost, complexity, and trade-offs when choosing the appropriate techniques, as different techniques may have different implications in terms of resource utilization, implementation effort, and maintenance overhead.

By implementing the techniques discussed in this section effectively, developers and administrators can optimize the performance and scalability of their chatbot or art generator systems, resulting in enhanced user experience, increased system efficiency, and improved customer satisfaction.

References:

Amazon Web Services (AWS). (n.d.). Autoscaling best practices. Retrieved from https://aws.amazon.com/autoscaling/best-practices/

Google Cloud Platform (GCP). (n.d.). Autoscaling best practices. Retrieved from https://cloud.google.com/architecture/best-practices-for-building-automatable-application-architectures#autoscaling

Microsoft Azure. (n.d.). Design and implement a resilient, scalable application. Retrieved from https://docs.microsoft.com/en-us/azure/architecture/guide/design-principles/scalability

Redis. (n.d.). Redis caching best practices. Retrieved from https://redis.io/topics/memory-optimization

MongoDB. (n.d.). Performance best practices. Retrieved from https://docs.mongodb.com/manual/administration/optimization/

Krishnamurthy, R. (2019). High performance Python. Packt Publishing Ltd.

Fowler, M. (2018). Patterns of enterprise application architecture. Addison-Wesley Professional.

Hunt, A., & Thomas, D. (2018). The pragmatic programmer: Your journey to mastery. Addison-Wesley Professional.

Jepsen, K. (2017). Designing data-intensive applications: The big ideas behind reliable, scalable, and maintainable systems. O'Reilly Media.

Neward, T. (2019). Architecting Modern Java EE Applications. O'Reilly Media.

Fowler, M., & North, D. (2009). Continuous Integration. Addison-Wesley Professional.

Cockcroft, A. (2014). "The" Netflix OSS Cloud Architecture. Netflix Tech Blog.

Lightbend. (n.d.). Reactive Systems: The Benefits of Responsive, Resilient, Elastic, and Message-Driven Applications. Retrieved from https://www.lightbend.com/research/reactive-systems-the-benefits-of-responsive-resilient-elastic-and-message-driven-applications

The Twelve-Factor App. (n.d.). Retrieved from https://12factor.net/

Section 4: Performance and Scalability Testing

In this section, we will delve into the importance of performance and scalability testing for chatbots or art generators. We will explore different testing techniques that can be used to ensure optimal performance and the ability to handle high levels of traffic. Topics such as load testing, stress testing, and capacity planning will be discussed in detail, along with guidance on how to conduct these tests effectively.

Performance and scalability testing are crucial steps in the development and optimization process of a chatbot or art generator. These tests help identify potential bottlenecks, vulnerabilities, and limitations in the system, and enable developers to proactively address these issues before deploying the system in a production environment. By conducting performance and scalability testing, developers can validate the system's performance under varying workloads, ensure efficient resource utilization, minimize response times, and enhance the overall user experience.

Load Testing-

Load testing is a type of performance testing that involves subjecting the chatbot or art generator to simulated workloads to evaluate its performance under normal and expected peak load conditions. The purpose of load testing is to determine how the system performs under various levels of concurrent user interactions, and to identify the maximum load that the system can handle while maintaining acceptable performance levels.

To conduct effective load testing, it is essential to define realistic and relevant test scenarios that mimic the expected production workload. This can be achieved by simulating different types of user interactions, such as text queries, voice inputs, image uploads, or other relevant actions, and measuring the system's response time, resource utilization, and error rates. Load testing tools and frameworks, such as JMeter, Gatling, or Locust, can be used to automate the load testing process and generate comprehensive performance reports.

During load testing, it is important to monitor various system metrics, such as CPU utilization, memory usage, network throughput, and response times, to identify any performance degradation, errors, or bottlenecks. The load testing process should be repeated with increasing load levels until the system reaches its maximum capacity or performance starts to degrade, allowing developers to determine the system's limitations and optimize its performance accordingly.

Stress Testing-

Stress testing is a type of performance testing that involves subjecting the chatbot or art generator to extreme workloads that exceed the system's expected capacity. The purpose of stress testing is to evaluate the system's performance and stability under extreme conditions and identify its breaking point.

Stress testing is typically used to assess the system's resilience, robustness, and ability to recover from unexpected situations, such as sudden spikes in user traffic, high volumes of concurrent requests, or resource shortages. Stress testing can help identify potential issues, such as memory leaks, resource contention, or application crashes, that may occur under extreme conditions and impact the system's performance and stability.

To conduct effective stress testing, it is important to simulate extreme workloads that go beyond the system's expected capacity, and monitor the system's performance and stability during and after the stress test. Stress testing tools and frameworks, such as Apache JMeter, LoadRunner, or Siege, can be used to generate high levels of concurrent requests, simulate different types of workloads, and measure the system's response time, error rates, and resource utilization.

Capacity Planning-

Capacity planning is a process of estimating the resources, such as CPU, memory, storage, and network bandwidth, required to support the expected workload of the chatbot or art generator system. Capacity planning helps ensure that the system has sufficient resources to handle the expected traffic without experiencing performance degradation or resource shortages.

To conduct effective capacity planning, it is important to understand the expected workload of the system, including the number of concurrent users, the types of user interactions, the frequency of requests, and the expected growth over time. By analyzing historical data, conducting load testing, and monitoring system metrics during normal operation, developers can estimate the system's resource requirements and plan for adequate capacity to meet future demands.

Capacity planning involves forecasting the system's resource needs based on historical data, growth projections, and performance benchmarks. It requires careful analysis of the system's performance metrics, such as CPU utilization, memory usage, storage consumption, and network throughput, to identify trends and patterns. By monitoring and analyzing these metrics, developers can identify resource bottlenecks and plan for additional resources as needed.

Capacity planning also involves considering factors such as redundancy, failover mechanisms, and scalability options to ensure that the system can handle unexpected spikes in traffic or hardware failures without significant performance degradation. This may involve implementing load balancing techniques, clustering, caching mechanisms, or using cloud-based resources for scalability and redundancy.

Performance and Scalability Testing Best Practices-

To conduct performance and scalability testing effectively, it is important to follow some best practices:

Define realistic and relevant test scenarios: Test scenarios should mimic the expected production workload and include different types of user interactions and actions that are relevant to the system's functionality.

Use appropriate tools and frameworks: Choose the right tools and frameworks for load testing, stress testing, and capacity planning based on the system's technology stack, scalability requirements, and testing goals.

Monitor system metrics: Continuously monitor system metrics during testing to identify performance degradation, errors, or bottlenecks. Use monitoring tools, logs, and performance counters to gather relevant data for analysis.

Analyze performance data: Analyze the performance data collected during testing to identify trends, patterns, and anomalies. Use data visualization, statistical analysis, and comparison with performance benchmarks to gain insights into the system's performance and resource utilization.

Iterative testing: Perform performance and scalability testing iteratively, starting from lower load levels and gradually increasing the load to identify the system's performance limits and optimize its performance accordingly.

Test in production-like environment: Test the system in an environment that closely resembles the production environment in terms of hardware, software, network configuration, and workload to ensure accurate results.

Test for peak loads: Test the system for peak loads to identify its maximum capacity and ensure that it can handle the expected traffic during peak usage periods.

Plan for scalability: Consider scalability options, such as vertical and horizontal scaling, load balancing, or auto-scaling, during performance and scalability testing to ensure that the system can handle future growth in traffic and users.

Analyze failures and errors: Analyze failures, errors, and performance degradation during testing to identify the root causes and take corrective actions. This may involve code optimization, database optimization, caching, or other performance tuning techniques.

Document and report findings: Document the testing process, results, and recommendations for performance and scalability optimization. Provide comprehensive reports to stakeholders, including developers, testers, project managers, and system administrators, for review and action.

Performance and scalability are critical factors for the success of chatbots or art generators. Optimizing performance and ensuring scalability requires careful consideration of various techniques, including caching, code optimization, database optimization, load balancing, vertical and horizontal scaling, and auto-scaling. Additionally, conducting performance and scalability testing using load testing, stress testing, and capacity planning techniques can help identify potential issues and optimize the system's performance under varying workloads.

By implementing these techniques effectively, developers can ensure that their chatbots or art generators deliver optimal performance, provide a seamless user experience, and can handle high levels of traffic and user interactions. Following best practices, analyzing performance data, and continuously optimizing the system based on test results can help achieve a robust, scalable, and high-performing chatbot or art generator system.

Section 5: Security and Privacy Considerations

In this section, we will explore the security and privacy considerations that come with optimizing performance and scalability. We will discuss topics such as data encryption, access control, and network security, and provide guidance on how to ensure that your chatbot or art generator is secure and compliant with relevant regulations.

In today's digital landscape, security and privacy are critical concerns for any software application, including chatbots or art generators. Optimizing performance and scalability must go hand-in-hand with ensuring that the system is secure, and sensitive user data is protected. In this section, we will delve into the security and privacy considerations that are essential to maintaining the integrity, confidentiality, and compliance of your chatbot or art generator.

Data Encryption-

Data encryption is a fundamental technique used to protect sensitive information from unauthorized access. Encryption involves converting data into a coded format that can only be deciphered with the appropriate encryption key. By encrypting data, even if it is intercepted or accessed without authorization, it remains unreadable and unusable.

To ensure the security of your chatbot or art generator, it is essential to implement strong encryption mechanisms for sensitive data, such as user inputs, authentication credentials, and other confidential information. This includes encrypting data both in transit and at rest.

For data in transit, use secure communication protocols, such as HTTPS, SSL, or TLS, to encrypt data as it travels over the network. This helps prevent eavesdropping, man-in-the-middle attacks, and data interception.

For data at rest, use industry-standard encryption algorithms, such as AES, to encrypt data stored in databases, files, or other storage systems. Implement proper key management practices, such as key rotation, storage, and access controls, to ensure the confidentiality and integrity of encryption keys.

Access Control-

Access control is a crucial aspect of ensuring the security and privacy of your chatbot or art generator. It involves managing and restricting access to system resources based on user roles, privileges, and permissions.

Implement robust authentication and authorization mechanisms to ensure that only authorized users can access the system and perform specific actions. Use strong authentication methods, such as multi-factor authentication (MFA), to enhance the security of user accounts and prevent unauthorized access.

Set up granular access controls that follow the principle of least privilege, where users are granted only the minimum permissions necessary to perform their tasks. Regularly review and update user permissions and roles to ensure that they are aligned with the principle of least privilege and reflect the current needs of the system.

Implement audit logs and monitoring mechanisms to track and monitor user activity, system access, and actions performed within the system. This helps detect and prevent any unauthorized access or malicious activities in real-time.

Network Security-

Network security is essential to protect your chatbot or art generator from external threats and attacks. Implement robust network security measures to safeguard against unauthorized access, data breaches, and other security risks.

Use firewalls, intrusion detection and prevention systems (IDPS), and virtual private networks (VPNs) to protect the network perimeter and prevent unauthorized access to the system. Configure firewalls to allow only necessary network traffic and block all other incoming and outgoing connections.

Regularly update and patch all software and hardware components of the system, including the operating system, web servers, libraries, and other dependencies. This helps address known security vulnerabilities and reduces the risk of exploitation by attackers.

Segment the network and limit the communication channels between different components of the system. This helps contain potential security breaches and prevents lateral movement by attackers within the system.

Implement network monitoring and logging mechanisms to track and detect any suspicious activities, such as port scanning, brute force attacks, or unusual traffic patterns. Use security information and event management (SIEM) tools to collect, analyze, and correlate logs from various system components for timely detection of security incidents.

Compliance with Regulations-

Compliance with relevant regulations and standards is crucial to ensure the privacy and security of user data in your chatbot or art generator. Depending on the industry and location, there may be specific regulations that you need to comply with, such as the General Data Protection Regulation (GDPR), Health Insurance Portability and Accountability Act (HIPAA), or Payment Card Industry Data Security Standard (PCI-DSS). It is important to thoroughly understand the regulatory requirements that apply to your chatbot or art generator and ensure that your system is designed and implemented in accordance with these regulations.

Implement appropriate data handling practices, such as data minimization, where only the necessary data is collected and stored, and data retention policies, where data is retained only for the required duration. Ensure that user consent is obtained before collecting any personal data and provide users with clear and transparent information about how their data will be used.

Implement proper mechanisms for user data protection, such as pseudonymization and anonymization, to reduce the risk of data breaches and protect user privacy. Pseudonymization involves replacing personally identifiable information (PII) with pseudonyms or codes, while anonymization involves removing any identifiable information from the data set.

Regularly conduct security audits and assessments to identify and address any vulnerabilities or weaknesses in your chatbot or art generator. Perform penetration testing and vulnerability scanning to identify potential security gaps and take necessary actions to remediate them.

Train your development team and system administrators on security best practices, such as secure coding techniques, secure configuration management, and incident response procedures. Implement a strong security culture within your organization, emphasizing the importance of security and privacy in all aspects of the system.

Privacy by Design and Default-

Privacy by Design and Default is a concept that promotes the integration of privacy and security considerations into the design, development, and operation of software applications. It focuses on proactively addressing privacy and security concerns from the very beginning of the system development process.

When optimizing the performance and scalability of your chatbot or art generator, it is important to ensure that privacy and security are considered as integral components of the system, rather than an afterthought. This includes incorporating privacy and security features during the system design phase, such as data encryption, access controls, and user consent mechanisms.

Implement privacy and security as default settings in your chatbot or art generator. Avoid collecting unnecessary personal data, limit access to sensitive data to only authorized users, and ensure that all default configurations are secure and comply with relevant regulations. Provide users with clear options to control their data and privacy settings, and make sure that these settings are easy to understand and configure.

Regular Security Monitoring and Incident Response-

Implement a robust security monitoring and incident response plan to detect, respond to, and mitigate security incidents in a timely manner. This includes monitoring system logs, network traffic, and user activity for any signs of suspicious behavior or security breaches.

Set up automated alerts and notifications for potential security incidents, such as failed login attempts, unusual data access patterns, or system anomalies. Establish a clear and well-defined incident response plan that includes procedures for identifying, escalating, and resolving security incidents.

Regularly review and update your incident response plan to reflect changes in the system, technology landscape, and regulatory requirements. Conduct post-incident analysis to identify root causes, vulnerabilities, and weaknesses in the system, and take necessary actions to remediate them.

Employee Awareness and Training-

Employees play a critical role in ensuring the security and privacy of your chatbot or art generator. It is important to provide regular awareness training to your employees to educate them about security best practices, the importance of data privacy, and the potential risks and threats to the system.

Train your employees on how to recognize and report security incidents, how to handle sensitive data, and how to follow security and privacy policies and procedures. Emphasize the need for strong passwords, regular password changes, and secure authentication practices.

Regularly reinforce the importance of security and privacy through ongoing training, reminders, and updates on the latest security threats and vulnerabilities.

Secure Network Communication-

Securing network communication is essential in protecting the privacy and security of your chatbot or art generator. Implement encryption protocols, such as Secure Socket Layer (SSL) or Transport Layer Security (TLS), to ensure that all data transmitted between the chatbot and other systems is encrypted and secure.

Use secure communication channels, such as Virtual Private Networks (VPNs), to transmit data securely over the internet. Restrict incoming and outgoing network traffic to only necessary ports and protocols, and implement firewalls and intrusion detection systems (IDS) to detect and prevent unauthorized access attempts.

Regularly monitor network traffic and system logs for any suspicious activity or anomalies, and take appropriate actions to investigate and address any potential security threats.

Access Control and Authentication-

Implement strong access controls to ensure that only authorized personnel have access to your chatbot or art generator. Use role-based access control (RBAC) mechanisms to assign permissions and privileges based on job responsibilities and restrict access to sensitive data or functionalities to only those who need it.

Implement multi-factor authentication (MFA) for all user accounts, including developers, system administrators, and users with access to the system. Require strong and unique passwords, and regularly enforce password changes to prevent unauthorized access.

Regularly review and update access privileges, revoke access for users who no longer require it, and disable or remove inactive accounts to minimize the risk of unauthorized access.

Regular Software Updates and Patching-

Keeping your software and systems up-to-date with the latest security patches and updates is critical in mitigating potential vulnerabilities and reducing the risk of security breaches. Regularly update your chatbot or art generator software, libraries, frameworks, and dependencies to ensure that known security vulnerabilities are patched.

Establish a process for regularly monitoring and applying software updates and patches, and test the system for any potential impact on performance or functionality. Stay informed about the latest security vulnerabilities and patches, and prioritize critical security updates.

Backups and Disaster Recovery-

Implement regular backups of your chatbot or art generator system and data to ensure that you can quickly recover from any data loss or system failure. Store backups in secure and offsite locations to protect against data breaches, ransomware attacks, or physical damage to the system.

Test the backup and disaster recovery process to ensure that it is working effectively and can be relied upon in case of an emergency. Develop a comprehensive disaster recovery plan that includes procedures for system restoration, data recovery, and communication with stakeholders in case of a security incident or system failure.

Optimizing the performance and scalability of your chatbot or art generator requires careful consideration of security and privacy considerations. By implementing strong data encryption, access controls, network security, and complying with relevant regulations, along with incorporating privacy and security as part of the system design and operation, regularly monitoring and updating the system, and providing employee awareness and training, you can ensure that your chatbot or art generator is secure and protected against potential security threats. By following best practices for security and privacy, you can build a robust and compliant system that instills trust and confidence in your users and stakeholders.

Section 6: Best Practices for Optimizing Performance and Scalability

In this section, we will cover some best practices for optimizing the performance and scalability of your chatbot or art generator. Implementing these best practices can help you ensure that your system performs optimally, can handle high levels of traffic, and provides a smooth and reliable experience for your users.

Monitoring and Logging-

Implement robust monitoring and logging mechanisms to gain insights into the performance and health of your chatbot or art generator system. Monitor key performance metrics such as response time, CPU usage, memory utilization, and error rates to detect any performance bottlenecks or issues.

Set up logging to capture important system events, errors, and exceptions for later analysis and troubleshooting. Log critical information such as user interactions, system errors, and performance data to help diagnose and resolve issues promptly.

Use monitoring and logging tools, such as logging frameworks, performance monitoring software, and error tracking solutions, to gain real-time visibility into the system's performance and identify areas that require optimization.

Error Handling-

Implement robust error handling mechanisms to handle unexpected errors and exceptions that may occur during the operation of your chatbot or art generator. Proper error handling can help prevent system crashes, data corruption, and negative user experiences.

Implement graceful error recovery strategies, such as retrying failed operations, rolling back transactions, or failing gracefully with meaningful error messages to users. Use appropriate error codes or error messages to provide clear and helpful information to users in case of errors.

Regularly review system logs and error reports to identify recurring errors and take corrective actions to address them. Continuously improve error handling mechanisms based on feedback from users and system monitoring to enhance system reliability and performance.

Version Control-

Implement version control best practices to manage the source code and configuration files of your chatbot or art generator system. Use version control software, such as Git or Subversion, to track changes, manage different versions, and collaborate with team members.

Create separate branches for different development tasks or features and follow a branching model that fits your development workflow, such as GitFlow or Feature Branching. Regularly merge changes from feature branches to the main branch and conduct thorough testing before deploying changes to production.

Maintain a release management process that includes version tagging, release notes, and rollback plans to ensure that only tested and approved changes are deployed to production. Keep track of dependencies, libraries, and third-party components used in your system and regularly update them to their latest stable versions to ensure security and performance.

Performance Optimization Techniques-

Implement performance optimization techniques to ensure that your chatbot or art generator system performs optimally and provides a responsive user experience. Here are some performance optimization best practices:

a. Caching: Use caching mechanisms, such as in-memory caching, distributed caching, or content delivery networks (CDNs), to cache frequently accessed data or computations and reduce the overhead of repetitive computations or database queries.

b. Code Optimization: Review and optimize your code to identify and resolve performance bottlenecks, such as slow database queries, CPU-intensive operations, or unnecessary computations. Optimize database queries, use lazy loading or pagination for fetching large data sets, and minimize unnecessary data transfers or computations.

c. Database Optimization: Optimize your database design, schema, indexing, and query performance to ensure efficient and fast data retrieval and manipulation. Use database caching, database sharding, or database partitioning techniques to distribute data across multiple servers and improve scalability.

d. Performance Testing: Conduct regular performance testing to identify and resolve performance issues before they impact the system's performance. Use load testing tools, stress testing tools, or performance monitoring solutions to simulate high levels of traffic and measure system performance under different load scenarios.

e. Resource Management: Optimize the usage of system resources, such as CPU, memory, and network bandwidth, to ensure efficient resource management and prevent resource contention. Avoid resource-intensive operations, unnecessary data transfers, or redundant computations that can impact the performance of your system.

Security and Privacy Considerations-

Ensure that your chatbot or art generator system is secure and compliant with relevant regulations by implementing appropriate security and privacy measures. Here are some best practices for security and privacy considerations:

a. Data Encryption: Use encryption techniques, such as SSL/TLS, to secure data transmission between clients and servers, and use encryption algorithms, such as AES, to encrypt sensitive data stored in databases or other storage systems.

b. Access Control: Implement strong access control mechanisms to ensure that only authorized users have access to your system and its resources. Use role-based access control (RBAC), multi-factor authentication (MFA), and other authentication and authorization mechanisms to protect against unauthorized access.

c. Network Security: Implement network security measures, such as firewalls, intrusion detection systems (IDS), and virtual private networks (VPNs), to protect your system from external threats. Regularly update and patch network devices and systems to protect against known vulnerabilities.

d. Regular Security Audits: Conduct regular security audits to identify and address potential security vulnerabilities in your system. Perform vulnerability assessments, penetration testing, and security code reviews to identify and fix security weaknesses and ensure that your system is secure against potential attacks.

e. Compliance with Regulations: Ensure that your chatbot or art generator system complies with relevant regulations, such as data privacy regulations (e.g., GDPR, HIPAA), industry standards, and security best practices. Regularly review and update your system to ensure compliance with changing regulations and standards.

Continuous Improvement-

Continuously monitor, evaluate, and improve the performance and scalability of your chatbot or art generator system. Regularly review system metrics, logs, and user feedback to identify areas that require optimization or improvement. Use automated testing, continuous integration, and continuous deployment practices to detect and fix performance or scalability issues in a timely manner.

Regularly update and patch dependencies, libraries, and third-party components used in your system to ensure security and performance. Stay up-to-date with the latest industry trends, best practices, and technologies related to performance and scalability optimization, security, and privacy, and implement them in your system as needed.

With that being said optimizing the performance and scalability of your chatbot or art generator system requires careful planning, monitoring, and implementation of best practices. By following the recommendations outlined in this section, you can ensure that your system performs optimally, can handle high levels of traffic, and provides a secure and reliable user experience.

Scaling Your Backend

Scaling your backend is a crucial step in ensuring that your chatbot or art generator can handle increasing traffic and remain responsive. There are several approaches to scaling, including vertical scaling and horizontal scaling. Vertical scaling involves adding more resources to a single server, such as increasing the amount of RAM or CPU power. This approach can be effective for small to medium-sized chatbots or art generators, but it has limitations in terms of how much it can scale.

Horizontal Scaling-

Horizontal scaling is a popular technique used to optimize the performance and scalability of systems, including chatbots or art generators. It involves adding more servers to distribute the workload, which allows the system to handle higher levels of traffic and achieve better scalability compared to vertical scaling, where resources are added to a single server. In this section, we will explore horizontal scaling in depth, including various implementation methods, examples, and a step-by-step guide for readers to work along with and try themselves.

Understanding Horizontal Scaling-

Horizontal scaling involves adding more servers to a system to handle increased workload and traffic. This approach distributes the load across multiple servers, allowing for better performance and scalability. As the workload increases, more servers can be added to the system to handle the additional load, ensuring that the system remains responsive and available.

Horizontal scaling can be achieved in several ways, including:

a. Load Balancing: Load balancing is the process of distributing incoming network traffic across multiple servers to prevent any one server from becoming a performance bottleneck. A load balancer acts as a traffic controller that distributes incoming requests to multiple servers based on predefined algorithms, such as round-robin, least connections, or IP hash. This evenly distributes the workload across the servers, ensuring that no single server is overwhelmed with too much traffic.

b. Sharding: Sharding is the process of partitioning a database or data storage system across multiple servers or nodes. Each shard contains a subset of data, and each server is responsible for handling a specific shard. This allows for parallel processing of data, which can significantly improve performance and scalability. Sharding can be implemented at the application level, where the application itself handles data partitioning, or at the database level, where the database system handles data partitioning.

c. Replication: Replication involves creating multiple copies of the same data on different servers. These copies are kept in sync with each other, ensuring that any changes made to one copy are replicated to the other copies. Replication can be used for both data redundancy and improved performance. For example, read-heavy workloads can be offloaded to replicas, reducing the load on the primary server and improving response times for read requests.

Examples of Horizontal Scaling Implementation-

Let's take a look at some examples of how horizontal scaling can be implemented in a chatbot or art generator system.

Example 1: Load Balancing

In this example, we will implement load balancing to distribute incoming traffic across multiple servers. The goal is to ensure that no single server becomes a performance bottleneck and that the system can handle high levels of traffic.

Step 1: Set up Multiple Servers

First, we need to set up multiple servers to handle the incoming traffic. These servers can be virtual machines or physical servers, depending on the requirements of the system. Each server should have the necessary software and dependencies installed to run the chatbot or art generator system.

Step 2: Install Load Balancer

Next, we need to install a load balancer that will distribute incoming traffic across the servers. There are several load balancing options available, such as hardware load balancers, software load balancers, or cloud-based load balancers. Choose the one that best fits your system's requirements.

Step 3: Configure Load Balancer

Once the load balancer is installed, we need to configure it to distribute incoming traffic across the servers. This typically involves setting up rules or algorithms to determine how traffic should be distributed, such as round-robin, least connections, or IP hash.

Step 4: Test and Monitor

After the load balancer is configured, it's important to thoroughly test the system to ensure that traffic is being distributed correctly and that the system is performing optimally. Monitor the system closely for any performance or scalability issues and make adjustments to the load balancer configuration as

Caching

Caching involves storing frequently accessed data in memory or on disk to reduce the amount of time it takes to retrieve that data. This can significantly improve the performance of your chatbot or art generator, especially for frequently accessed data like user profiles or frequently used responses.

There are several types of caching that can be used in chatbots and art generators, including in-memory caching, disk caching, and distributed caching. In-memory caching involves storing data in the RAM of your server, which can be accessed much faster than disk storage. Disk caching involves storing data on disk to reduce the amount of time it takes to retrieve that data. Distributed caching involves storing data across multiple servers to improve performance and scalability.

Tools like Redis and Memcached can be used to implement caching in your chatbot or art generator. These tools provide fast, scalable caching that can significantly improve the performance of your tool.

Monitoring and Logging

Monitoring and logging are essential for ensuring the performance and availability of your chatbot or art generator. Monitoring involves tracking key performance indicators (KPIs) like response time, throughput, and error rate to identify potential issues and improve performance. Logging involves recording detailed information about requests and responses to help diagnose issues and improve functionality.

Tools like Prometheus and Grafana can be used to monitor the performance of your chatbot or art generator, while tools like Elasticsearch and Logstash can be used to log requests and responses.

Vertical Scaling-

Section: Vertical Scaling - Optimizing Performance and Scalability

In this section, we help understand the process of vertical scaling, which involves increasing the resources of a single server or node to optimize the performance and scalability of a chatbot or art generator system. We will explore the various methods of vertical scaling, including increasing CPU, memory, and storage capacity, and provide guidance on best practices to implement vertical scaling effectively.

Methods of Vertical Scaling-

There are several methods to implement vertical scaling, depending on the requirements and constraints of the system. Some common methods of vertical scaling include:

a. Increasing CPU Capacity: This involves upgrading the CPU of a server to a more powerful one with higher clock speed or more cores. This allows for better processing power, which can handle higher levels of traffic and workload.

b. Increasing Memory Capacity: This involves upgrading the memory (RAM) of a server to a higher capacity. This allows for better data processing and caching, which can improve system performance and handle larger data sets.

c. Increasing Storage Capacity: This involves upgrading the storage capacity of a server, such as adding more hard drives or SSDs. This allows for storing more data, such as user profiles, images, or other content, which can improve system responsiveness and scalability.

Step-by-Step Guide for Vertical Scaling-

Implementing vertical scaling requires careful planning and execution to ensure that the system resources are effectively utilized and the desired performance and scalability improvements are achieved. Here's a step-by-step guide for implementing vertical scaling:

Step 1: Identify Resource Bottlenecks

First, identify the resource bottlenecks in the chatbot or art generator system by monitoring and analyzing system performance metrics. This could involve checking CPU utilization, memory usage, storage capacity, and other relevant metrics to identify the resources that are limiting system performance.

Step 2: Determine Resource Upgrade Requirements

Based on the identified resource bottlenecks, determine the specific resource upgrade requirements. This could involve upgrading the CPU, memory, or storage capacity, or a combination of these resources, based on the system's needs and constraints.

Step 3: Plan and Execute Resource Upgrades

Next, plan and execute the resource upgrades in a controlled and organized manner. This could involve coordinating with hardware vendors or cloud service providers to upgrade the CPU, memory, or storage capacity of the server or node.

Step 4: Test and Monitor

After the resource upgrades are implemented, thoroughly test the system to ensure that the performance and scalability improvements are achieved. Monitor the system closely for any performance issues or resource utilization anomalies and make adjustments as needed.

Best Practices for Vertical Scaling-

To ensure optimal performance and scalability with vertical scaling, it's important to follow best practices. Some of the best practices for vertical scaling include:

a. Capacity Planning: Perform thorough capacity planning to determine the appropriate resource upgrades based on system requirements, workload projections, and performance metrics. This ensures that the right amount of resources are added to handle the anticipated workload.

b. Performance Monitoring: Implement comprehensive performance monitoring mechanisms to track system performance, resource utilization, and potential bottlenecks. This allows for proactive identification and resolution of performance issues and ensures that the system is utilizing the added resources effectively.

c. Backup and Recovery: Implement robust backup and recovery mechanisms to ensure data integrity and system availability during resource upgrades or in case of any failures. This protects the system against data loss and minimizes downtime during upgrades.

d. Testing and Validation: Thoroughly test the system after resource upgrades to ensure that the expected performance and scalability improvements are achieved. This could involve load testing, stress testing, and performance benchmarking to validate the system's capabilities and identify any potential issues.

e. Scalability Planning: Consider future scalability needs while implementing vertical scaling. Plan for additional resource upgrades as the system continues to grow and handle higher levels of traffic. This ensures that the system remains scalable in the long run and can handle increasing workload demands.

f. Automation: Automate the resource upgrade process as much as possible to minimize human errors and ensure consistency. Use configuration management tools or infrastructure-as-code techniques to automate resource provisioning, configuration, and deployment.

Examples of Vertical Scaling-

Let's take an example of a chatbot system that is experiencing performance issues due to high CPU utilization. To address this bottleneck, the system administrator decides to implement vertical scaling by upgrading the CPU of the server. Here's a step-by-step example guide for implementing vertical scaling in this scenario:

Step 1: Identify Resource Bottleneck

The system administrator monitors the system performance metrics and identifies that the CPU utilization is consistently high, causing performance degradation of the chatbot system.

Step 2: Determine Resource Upgrade Requirements

Based on the resource bottleneck, the system administrator determines that upgrading the CPU of the server is required to improve system performance.

Step 3: Plan and Execute CPU Upgrade

The system administrator plans the CPU upgrade, selects a more powerful CPU with higher clock speed and more cores, and coordinates with the hardware vendor to install the new CPU on the server.

Step 4: Test and Monitor

After the CPU upgrade, the system administrator thoroughly tests the system to ensure that the expected performance improvements are achieved. The system is monitored closely for any performance issues or anomalies.

Vertical scaling can be an effective approach to optimize the performance and scalability of a chatbot or art generator system by adding more resources to a single server or node. By upgrading the CPU, memory, or storage capacity, vertical scaling can help the system handle higher levels of traffic and workload. Following best practices, such as capacity planning, performance monitoring, backup and recovery, testing and validation, scalability planning, and automation, can ensure that the vertical scaling process is executed effectively. By considering the specific requirements and constraints of the system, vertical scaling can be a viable solution for improving the performance and scalability of a chatbot or art generator system.

Chapter 8: Testing and Deployment

Once you have built and optimized your chatbot or art generator, the next step is to test and deploy it. Proper testing is essential to ensure that your tool is functioning correctly and meeting the needs of your users, while proper deployment is necessary to make your tool available to the world. In this chapter, we will cover the best practices for testing and deploying your tool, including how to write effective test cases, how to use automated testing tools, and how to deploy your tool to a server.

Testing Your Tool

Testing is a critical part of the development process for any software application, including chatbots and art generators. There are many different types of testing that you can perform, including unit testing, integration testing, and acceptance testing. Here, we will focus on acceptance testing, which is the process of verifying that your tool meets the requirements and expectations of your users.

Before you start testing your tool, it is essential to define your test cases. A test case is a set of steps or conditions that a user would follow to achieve a specific outcome. For example, a test case for a chatbot might involve asking the chatbot a specific question and verifying that it provides the correct response.

When writing test cases, it is essential to consider all possible scenarios that a user might encounter. This includes both normal and edge cases, such as unexpected user input or errors in the backend code. It is also important to test your tool on different devices, browsers, and operating systems to ensure that it is compatible with a wide range of user environments.

Once you have defined your test cases, you can begin testing your tool. One effective way to test your tool is to use automated testing tools. These tools can help you test your tool more quickly and efficiently than manual testing. There are many different types of automated testing tools available, including Selenium, Cypress, and Appium.

Selenium is a popular open-source tool for automating web applications. It allows you to write test scripts in multiple programming languages, such as Python, JavaScript, and Java. Selenium can be used to simulate user actions, such as clicking on buttons and entering text, and verify that your tool responds correctly.

Cypress is another popular testing tool that is specifically designed for testing web applications. It provides an easy-to-use interface for writing and executing tests, and it includes features such as real-time reloading and interactive debugging.

Appium is a tool that is specifically designed for testing mobile applications. It allows you to write test scripts in multiple programming languages, such as Python, JavaScript, and Java, and it provides a range of testing capabilities, such as simulating user gestures and verifying UI elements.

User testing is another essential part of the testing process. User testing involves gathering feedback from real users to identify any issues or areas for improvement in your tool. This feedback can be collected through surveys, interviews, or user testing sessions. User testing can help you identify usability issues, such as confusing user interfaces or unresponsive chatbot responses, and it can also help you identify bugs or errors that you may not have noticed during your own testing.

Deploying Your Tool

Once you have thoroughly tested your tool and are confident that it is functioning correctly, it is time to deploy it to a server so that it can be accessed by users. There are many different hosting providers and deployment tools available, each with its own advantages and disadvantages.

One popular hosting provider is Amazon Web Services (AWS), which provides a range of services, such as Elastic Compute Cloud (EC2), Simple Storage Service (S3), and Lambda. AWS is known for its scalability and reliability, and it provides a range of tools for managing and deploying your applications.

Another popular hosting provider is Microsoft Azure, which provides a range of services, such as Virtual Machines,

User Acceptance Testing (UAT)

User Acceptance Testing (UAT) is the final stage of testing before a chatbot or art generator is released to the public. In UAT, the chatbot or art generator is tested by actual end-users to ensure that it meets their needs and works as intended. This type of testing can provide valuable feedback on the user experience and identify any bugs or issues that may have been missed in previous testing stages. It is important to involve a diverse group of end-users in UAT to ensure that the tool is accessible and effective for all types of users.

Deployment

Once the testing process is complete, the chatbot or art generator is ready to be deployed to a hosting environment. This involves setting up a server and transferring the code and any required dependencies to the server. There are several hosting providers available, including cloud providers like Amazon Web Services (AWS) or Microsoft Azure, and managed hosting providers like Heroku or DigitalOcean. The choice of hosting provider will depend on factors like cost, scalability, and required features.

It is important to ensure that the deployed tool is secure and protected from potential attacks. This can be achieved by using security best practices like encryption, firewalls, and secure authentication methods. Additionally, it is important to regularly monitor the tool for any security vulnerabilities and patch them as soon as possible.

Conclusion

Testing and deployment are essential stages in the development process of a chatbot or art generator. Thorough testing can ensure that the tool meets user needs and works as intended, while effective deployment can ensure that the tool is accessible and secure. By following best practices in testing and deployment, developers can ensure that their chatbots and art generators are successful and meet the needs of their users.

Chapter 9: Best Practices and Future Trends

As chatbots and art generators become increasingly popular, it is important to stay up to date with best practices and emerging trends in development. This chapter will cover some of the best practices for chatbot and art generator development, as well as future trends in the field.

Best Practices in Chatbot Development

Design for User Experience

When developing a chatbot, it is important to design for user experience. This means creating a chatbot that is easy to use, intuitive, and provides value to the user. Some best practices for designing a chatbot with a good user experience include:

- Keeping the chatbot's purpose and capabilities clear from the beginning of the conversation.
- Creating a chatbot that is easy to navigate and understand, with a clear structure and intuitive design.
- Incorporating interactive elements, like buttons and quick replies, to help guide the user through the conversation.
- Making sure that the chatbot responds quickly and effectively to user input, with clear and concise messages.

Optimize for Performance

To provide a good user experience, your chatbot must be optimized for performance. Some best practices for optimizing chatbot performance include:

- Reducing response times by optimizing code and minimizing

API requests.

- Implementing caching and load balancing to ensure that the chatbot can handle high levels of traffic.
- Conducting regular load testing to identify and address performance bottlenecks.

Protect User Privacy

Protecting user privacy is crucial in chatbot development. Some best practices for protecting user privacy include:

- Collecting only the minimum amount of data necessary to provide the chatbot's services.
- Being transparent about data collection and use, and obtaining user consent for data collection.
- Implementing encryption and other security measures to protect user data.

Incorporate Machine Learning and NLP

Incorporating machine learning and natural language processing (NLP) can help your chatbot understand user input and generate relevant responses. Some best practices for incorporating machine learning and NLP include:

- Choosing the right machine learning framework and training data for your chatbot's needs.
- Regularly updating and retraining your chatbot's machine learning models to ensure that they stay accurate and relevant.
- Incorporating NLP libraries like spaCy or NLTK to help your chatbot understand natural language input.

Future Trends in Chatbot Development

Virtual Assistants

Virtual assistants are chatbots that can perform a variety of tasks, from scheduling appointments to providing weather updates. In the future, virtual assistants are expected to become even more sophisticated and capable, with the ability to handle complex tasks and provide personalized recommendations based on user data.

Integration with Augmented Reality

As augmented reality (AR) technology becomes more prevalent, chatbots are expected to become more integrated with AR experiences. For example, a chatbot could provide users with information about products or landmarks they encounter in an AR environment.

Improved Natural Language Understanding

Advances in natural language processing are expected to make chatbots more effective at understanding and responding to user input. This could involve incorporating more sophisticated machine learning models or integrating chatbots with other technologies like voice recognition.

Increased Use in Healthcare and Education

Chatbots are already being used in healthcare and education to provide personalized support and guidance to patients and students. In the future, chatbots are expected to become even more prevalent in these fields, helping to improve outcomes and reduce costs.

As chatbots and art generators continue to grow in popularity, it is essential to stay up to date with best practices and emerging trends in development. By designing for user experience, optimizing for performance, protecting user privacy, and incorporating machine learning and NLP, you can create effective and useful chatbots. Additionally, by keeping an eye on emerging

Final Thoughts

As technology continues to advance, chatbots and art generators will likely play an increasingly important role in various fields, from customer service to entertainment to education. By learning how to build and deploy these tools, you can position yourself at the forefront of this exciting and rapidly evolving field.

Throughout this book, we have covered a range of topics and provided numerous resources to help you along the way. Whether you are a seasoned developer or a newcomer to programming, there is something in this book for everyone. By selecting the right programming language, designing a user-friendly interface, incorporating machine learning and NLP, optimizing for performance and scalability, and thoroughly testing and deploying your tool, you can create a chatbot or art generator that is both functional and aesthetically pleasing.

Of course, there is always more to learn, and the world of chatbots and art generators is constantly evolving. As you continue to develop your skills in this field, we encourage you to stay up to date on the latest trends and best practices. Below are some resources to help you get started:

TensorFlow: A popular open-source machine learning framework developed by Google.

Keras: A high-level neural networks API that runs on top of TensorFlow.

NLTK: A leading platform for building NLP systems in Python.

spaCy: An advanced NLP library for Python and Cython.

Selenium: A powerful tool for automating web browser interactions.

Cypress: A JavaScript-based end-to-end testing framework.

Docker: A containerization platform that simplifies application deployment.

Kubernetes: An open-source container orchestration platform for automating deployment, scaling, and management of containerized applications.

AWS: Amazon Web Services offers a range of hosting and deployment solutions for chatbots and art generators.

GCP: Google Cloud Platform provides hosting, storage, and other cloud services for chatbots and art generators.

By leveraging these tools and staying up to date on the latest developments in the field, you can continue to push the boundaries of what is possible with chatbots and art generators. We wish you the best of luck on your journey and hope that this book has provided a useful starting point for your own projects.

As you continue on your journey of building chatbots and art generators, it is important to stay up to date on the latest trends and developments in the field. By participating in online communities, attending conferences and workshops, and reading industry publications, you can stay informed about new tools, techniques, and applications for chatbots and art generators. Additionally, by keeping an eye on emerging technologies like virtual assistants, natural language processing, and machine learning, you can stay ahead of the curve and continue to push the boundaries of what is possible with chatbots and art generators.

Building a chatbot or art generator is a challenging but rewarding endeavor. By following the best practices outlined in this book and staying informed about the latest trends and developments in the field, you can create a tool that is both technically sound and visually striking. So go forth, experiment, and create something amazing!

The Ai Prompting Bible
By: Michael Ferguson

Chapter 1: Introduction

Welcome to the Self-Help AI Prompting Journal, where creativity meets innovation! In this chapter, we'll dive into the nitty-gritty details of what this journal is all about, how to use it to unlock your creative genius, and some tips and tricks to make the most out of the prompts. So, buckle up and get ready for a wild ride of self-discovery and artistic exploration!

About the Journal: This journal is not your ordinary run-of-the-mill notebook. It's a cutting-edge tool that combines the power of artificial intelligence with the limitless potential of your creative mind. With a treasure trove of AI-generated prompts, ranging from writing to drawing to mind-bending AI-generated art, this journal is your personal muse on steroids. Whether you're an aspiring writer, a budding artist, or just someone looking to flex their creative muscles, this journal is your ultimate companion on the journey of self-expression.

How to Use this Journal: Using this journal is a piece of cake! All you need is an open mind, a sense of adventure, and a pen or pencil (or a stylus if you're tech-savvy). Simply flip through the pages, pick a prompt that catches your fancy, and let your imagination run wild. You can write, draw, or even code your way to artistic greatness with the prompts provided. There's no right or wrong way to use this journal, so feel free to experiment and make it your own. Embrace the unexpected and let your creativity soar to new heights!

Tips for Getting the Most out of the Prompts: Now, let's talk about some pro-tips to supercharge your creative journey with this journal. First and foremost, don't be afraid to take risks and step out of your comfort zone. The prompts are designed to push your boundaries and inspire you to think outside the box. So, be bold and embrace the unknown!

Secondly, don't worry about perfection. Remember, this journal is all about the process, not the end result. Let go of any inhibitions or self-doubt and let your creativity flow freely. Don't be afraid to make mistakes, as they can often lead to breakthroughs and unexpected discoveries.

Lastly, have fun and let your personality shine through. Inject your unique voice, style, and sense of humor into your writing, drawing, or coding. Be witty, be quirky, be you! After all, creativity is all about self-expression and having a blast along the way.

So, gear up and get ready to embark on a creative adventure like no other with the Self-Help AI Prompting Journal. Unleash your imagination, explore your artistic talents, and let the prompts be your guiding star on this exhilarating journey of self-discovery!

Stay tuned for Chapter 2, where we'll dive into the world of writing prompts and unlock the power of personal reflection, storytelling, and creative writing. Get ready to wield your pen like a creative ninja and unleash your wordsmith wizardry upon the pages of this journal! Let's do this!

Chapter 2: Writing Prompts

Welcome to the creative realm of writing prompts! In this chapter, we'll explore the diverse world of personal reflection prompts, storytelling prompts, and creative writing prompts. From introspective musings to epic tales and everything in between, get ready to embark on a literary adventure like no other!

Personal Reflection Prompts: Writing can be a cathartic and introspective experience, allowing you to delve deep into your thoughts, emotions, and memories. Personal reflection prompts are designed to help you gain insight into yourself, your life, and your experiences. They serve as a mirror that reflects your inner world onto the pages of the journal.

As you flip through the prompts, you might come across questions like:

What is a childhood memory that still impacts you today? Describe it in detail and reflect on its significance in your life.

Write a letter to your future self, describing your dreams, hopes, and aspirations. What advice would you give to your future self?

Describe a challenging situation you recently faced and how you dealt with it. What did you learn from that experience?

These prompts encourage you to pause, reflect, and explore your thoughts and emotions. They provide a safe space for you to express yourself openly and honestly. You can use them as a tool for self-discovery, gaining clarity, and processing your feelings. Feel free to pour your heart out onto the pages, and let your words be a vessel for self-expression.

Storytelling Prompts: If you've ever dreamt of being a master storyteller, this section is for you! Storytelling prompts are an invitation to embark on a literary journey and create your own unique tales. From fantasy realms to sci-fi adventures, from heartwarming anecdotes to thrilling mysteries, let your imagination run wild and weave your own stories.

Here are some examples of storytelling prompts:

Start a story with the sentence: "Once upon a time, in a land far, far away, there was a curious creature with purple fur and three tails."

Write a story about a young girl who discovers a hidden portal in her attic that leads to a magical world filled with talking animals and enchanted forests.

Create a story where the main character wakes up one day with a superpower they never knew they had, and the challenges they face as they navigate their newfound abilities.

These prompts are designed to challenge your creativity, ignite your storytelling skills, and transport you to a world of endless possibilities. You can experiment with different genres, settings, and characters. Let your words paint vivid imagery and immerse yourself in the joy of storytelling.

Creative Writing Prompts: If you're a wordsmith who loves to play with language, this section is for you! Creative writing prompts are designed to push the boundaries of your writing skills and inspire you to explore new forms of expression. From poetry to prose, from experimental writing to wordplay, let your words dance on the pages and create literary masterpieces.

Here are some examples of creative writing prompts:

Write a poem that captures the beauty of a sunrise without using any visual cues. Focus on the sounds, smells, and sensations that accompany the dawn.

Craft a short story using only dialogue between two characters who are stuck in an elevator during a power outage.

Create a piece of flash fiction in exactly 100 words that tells a complete story with a beginning, middle, and end.

These prompts challenge you to think critically, experiment with different writing styles, and push the boundaries of your creativity. You can play with words, experiment with form, and let your writing become a canvas for artistic expression. Don't be afraid to take risks, break rules, and explore new horizons with your writing.

Writing with Wit and Personality: Now, let's add a touch of wit and personality to your writing prompts! After all, creativity thrives on humor and individuality. So, as you embark on this literary journey, don't hesitate to infuse your writing with your unique sense of humor and personality. Let your prompts reflect your quirks, interests, and passions, and make them truly your own.

For instance, imagine a prompt like this:

Write a hilarious story about a mischievous unicorn who can't stop pranking the other magical creatures in the enchanted forest, but learns an important lesson about kindness along the way.

Or how about this one:

Describe a day in the life of a superhero whose superpower is the ability to control the weather, but struggles with keeping a good hair day in the midst of saving the world from villains.

With witty and personality-driven prompts like these, you can inject humor, sarcasm, and clever wordplay into your writing. It's an opportunity to let your creativity shine and make your writing truly unique and enjoyable.

Tips for Getting the Most out of the Prompts:

Embrace the Unexpected: Don't be afraid to take risks and think outside the box with your writing prompts. Embrace the unexpected and let your imagination run wild. The more you push the boundaries of your creativity, the more you'll discover new ideas and possibilities.

Make it Personal: Use the prompts as a platform to express yourself authentically. Infuse your writing with your own experiences, emotions, and perspectives. It's your opportunity to connect with your innermost thoughts and let your voice shine through.

Play with Different Genres: Don't limit yourself to one genre. Experiment with different writing styles, tones, and genres. Try your hand at poetry, fiction, non-fiction, or even hybrid forms of writing. It's a chance to explore your versatility and expand your writing skills.

Edit and Revise: Writing prompts are meant to be a starting point, not the final destination. After you've completed a piece of writing based on a prompt, take the time to edit and revise it. Polish your work, refine your language, and make it the best version of itself.

Have Fun with It: Remember, the purpose of this journal is to spark creativity and inspire you to have fun with your writing. Don't take it too seriously, and don't be afraid to let loose and enjoy the process. Allow yourself to play, experiment, and create without limitations.

So, grab your favorite pen or fire up your keyboard, and get ready to embark on a writing adventure like no other. Let the prompts be your guiding stars as you navigate the vast landscape of your imagination, and let your wit and personality shine through in your writing.

Now, let's move on to the next section of the journal, where we'll explore the world of drawing prompts and unleash our artistic talents on the blank canvas! Get your pencils, pens, or brushes ready, and let's dive in!

Chapter 3: Unleashing Your Artistic Talents - Drawing Prompts

Welcome to the world of drawing prompts! In this section of the journal, we will explore various drawing prompts that will inspire you to pick up your pencils, pens, or brushes and create art that is uniquely yours. Whether you are a seasoned artist or just starting out, these prompts will ignite your creativity and help you unlock new levels of artistic expression.

Drawing is a powerful form of communication and self-expression. It allows you to convey emotions, tell stories, and share your perspective with the world. With the right prompts, you can tap into your imagination and bring your ideas to life on the canvas. So, let us dive in and discover the magic of drawing prompts!

Sketching Prompts: From Quick Doodles to Detailed Illustrations

Sketching is a versatile form of drawing that can range from quick doodles to detailed illustrations. It is a wonderful way to capture your ideas and bring them to life on paper. With the following prompts, you will be able to explore different subjects, styles, and techniques, and create sketches that reflect your unique artistic vision.

Sketch a scene from your favorite childhood memory and add a twist to it that you wish had happened.

Create a sketch that depicts your dream travel destination, with all the sights and sounds that you imagine experiencing there.

Sketch a portrait of a person who has inspired you in your life and capture their essence and personality through your artistic interpretation.

Draw a still life of objects that hold sentimental value to you and use shading and texture to bring out their unique characteristics.

Create a character design for a fantastic creature that does not exist in the real world, and let your imagination run wild as you bring it to life on paper.

Doodling Prompts: Let Your Pen Roam Freely

Doodling is a spontaneous and intuitive form of drawing that allows your pen to roam freely on the paper without any constraints. It's a fun and liberating way to explore your creativity and create unique artworks that reflect your inner world. The following prompts will inspire you to let go of perfectionism and embrace the joy of doodling.

Start with a single line on the paper and let it guide you as you create a doodle that tells a story or conveys an emotion.

Close your eyes and use your non-dominant hand to create a doodle that represents how you are feeling in the moment, without lifting your pen from the paper.

Doodle a maze or a labyrinth and challenge yourself to find a way out by drawing a path through it.

Create a doodle that incorporates words or quotes that are meaningful to you and use the shapes and lines to convey their essence visually.

Doodle a scene from your favorite book or movie and add your own imaginative twists to it that make it uniquely yours.

Art Technique Prompts: Expand Your Artistic Horizons

Art techniques are the tools and methods that artists use to create their artworks. They can range from traditional techniques like watercolor, oil painting, or charcoal, to digital techniques like digital painting or mixed media. With the following prompts, you'll be able to expand your artistic horizons and experiment with different techniques to create artworks that push the boundaries of your creativity.

Experiment with a new art technique that you have always been curious about but have not tried before, such as printmaking, collage, or encaustic.

Create a mixed media artwork by combining different art techniques and materials, such as acrylic painting with collage, or watercolor with ink.

Use unconventional tools or materials to create your artwork, such as a toothbrush, a credit card, or even food items like coffee grounds or spices as a medium.

Explore the concept of negative space in your drawing, where you focus on the areas around the subject to create a visually captivating composition.

Experiment with different textures and surfaces in your artwork, such as using a palette knife to create thick impasto effects or using sandpaper to create a distressed or aged look.

Create a monochromatic artwork using only one color, and explore how different shades, tones, and values of that color can create depth and dimension in your drawing.

Challenge yourself to create an artwork using only simple geometric shapes and see how you can use them to create complex and intriguing compositions.

Try your hand at a unique style of art that you have never explored before, such as abstract, impressionistic, or surrealistic, and see how it influences your artistic expression.

Drawing prompts are not only about the result, but also about the process of creating. Embrace the journey of exploring different techniques, styles, and subjects, and allow yourself to make mistakes and learn from them. Remember, there are no rules in art, and the beauty of it lies in the freedom to express yourself in your own unique way.

Now, grab your pencils, pens, or brushes, and let your imagination run wild as you embark on an artistic adventure with these drawing prompts. Embrace the joy of doodling, the excitement of trying new techniques, and the satisfaction of creating artworks that reflect your inner world. Do not be afraid to push the boundaries of your creativity and discover new aspects of your artistic talents. So, let us get drawing and see where your artistic journey takes you!

Jokes and Witty Personality:

As we embark on this artistic adventure together, remember that drawing is like a magic wand that can bring your ideas to life on paper. It is like having your own superhero powers, but instead of saving the world, you get to create your own world with pencils and pens! So, put on your artistic cape and let us soar into the realm of drawing prompts!

And hey, if you are feeling a little "sketchy" about your drawing skills, do not worry! We all start somewhere, and the journey is half the fun. Just remember that even the greatest artists were once beginners who scribbled their first doodles. So, let go of perfectionism and embrace the quirks and imperfections in your drawings. After all, they are what make your artworks uniquely yours!

Now, I know what you're thinking - "But I can only draw stick figures!" Well, guess what? Stick figures are awesome! They are simple, cute, and can convey emotions and stories in their own unique way. So, do not be afraid to embrace your inner stick figure artist and let them take center stage in your drawings. Who knows, you might just become the Picasso of stick figures!

And remember, art is not just about the result, but also about the process. So, do not be afraid to get messy, try new techniques, and make bold artistic choices. If your drawing looks nothing like what you had in mind, just go with the flow, and see where it takes you. After all, some of the greatest masterpieces were created by happy accidents and serendipitous moments of inspiration.

So, grab your drawing tools, put on your creative hat, and let us dive into the world of drawing prompts with gusto! Whether you are a seasoned artist or a doodle enthusiast, these prompts are designed to spark your creativity and help you discover new aspects of your artistic talents. So, let us make some "art-tastic" masterpieces together!

As you have journeyed through the world of drawing prompts, I hope you have discovered

new techniques, styles, and subjects that have ignited your creativity and inspired you to create unique and captivating artworks. Drawing prompts are a wonderful way to explore your artistic skills, push your boundaries, and unlock your creative potential.

Remember, there are no right or wrong answers in art. Art is a form of self-expression, and each artist has their own unique voice and perspective. Embrace your individuality, experiment with different mediums and techniques, and let your imagination run wild on the canvas or paper.

Drawing prompts can also be a great tool for overcoming creative blocks or artist's block. If you are feeling stuck or uninspired, trying out a new drawing prompt can help you break free from your creative rut and reignite your passion for art. The prompts can provide a fresh perspective, challenge you to think freely, and spark innovative ideas and inspiration.

Furthermore, drawing prompts are not limited to just traditional drawing techniques. You can also use them as a springboard for exploring other forms of art, such as digital art, mixed media, collage, or even three-dimensional art. The possibilities are endless, and drawing prompts can serve as a launching pad for exploring different art forms and expanding your artistic horizons.

Drawing is not only about creating visually appealing artworks, but it is also a process of self-expression and personal growth. As you embark on your artistic journey with drawing prompts, you may discover new facets of yourself, your emotions, and your perspectives. Art has the power to evoke emotions, convey stories, and communicate messages, and drawing prompts can be a powerful tool for introspection and self-reflection.

In addition, drawing prompts can also be a wonderful way to connect with others and build a community of fellow artists. You can participate in drawing challenges or share your artworks on social media or online art forums and connect with other artists who share the same passion for creativity. Collaborations, feedback, and discussions with other artists can provide valuable insights, inspiration, and support on your artistic journey.

As you continue to explore drawing prompts and engage in your artistic practice, remember to be patient with yourself and allow yourself to make mistakes. Art is a continuous learning process, and every artwork you create is a steppingstone towards improvement and growth. Embrace the imperfections and enjoy the process of creation, without getting too caught up in perfectionism or self-criticism.

In conclusion, drawing prompts are a valuable tool for artists of all skill levels to explore their creativity, experiment with different techniques and mediums, overcome creative blocks, and connect with others. They provide endless possibilities for self-expression, personal growth, and artistic exploration. So, grab your pencils, pens, or brushes, and let your imagination soar as you embark on an artistic adventure with drawing prompts. Happy drawing!

Chapter 4: AI-Generated Art Prompts

Welcome to the exciting world of AI-generated art prompts! In this chapter, we will explore a fascinating intersection between art and technology, where artificial intelligence (AI) takes center stage as a creative collaborator. AI-generated art prompts offer a unique and innovative approach to sparking creativity, providing artists with fresh and unexpected prompts that can inspire new artistic directions and push the boundaries of traditional art.

Artificial intelligence has rapidly evolved in recent years, and its impact on the world of art has been profound. From generating art based on complex algorithms to creating unique visual and auditory experiences, AI has opened new possibilities for artists to explore and experiment with. AI-generated art prompts offer a cutting-edge and futuristic approach to creativity, where artists can harness the power of technology to fuel their artistic expression.

Visual Experience Prompts

One of the fascinating ways that AI-generated art prompts can inspire artists is through visual experience prompts. These prompts often involve using AI algorithms to generate visually stimulating images or designs that can serve as a starting point for an artwork. The images may be abstract, surreal, or hyper-realistic, and they can ignite the artist's imagination and spark ideas for new compositions, color palettes, or visual narratives.

Visual experience prompts can also push artists to experiment with unconventional techniques or mediums, as the AI-generated images may not adhere to traditional artistic norms. For example, an AI-generated visual experience prompt may combine digital and analog mediums, or incorporate unique textures, patterns, or visual effects that challenge the artist's perception of what is possible in art. This can lead to innovative and boundary-pushing creations that push the envelope of traditional art forms.

Furthermore, visual experience prompts can also encourage artists to explore different genres, styles, or themes that they may not have considered before. The AI-generated images may present unexpected visual juxtapositions or combinations, leading artists to explore new artistic genres, cultural references, or visual storytelling techniques. This can expand the artist's artistic horizons and open up new creative avenues for exploration.

Audio Experience Prompts

Another intriguing aspect of AI-generated art prompts is the integration of auditory experiences into the creative process. AI algorithms can generate unique and immersive soundscapes, music, or other auditory stimuli that can serve as prompts for artistic creation. These audio experience prompts can inspire artists to explore the relationship between sound and visual art, and how they can be combined to create multisensory artworks.

Audio experience prompts can challenge artists to think beyond the visual aspects of art and consider how sound can enhance or alter the perception of an artwork. For example, an AI-generated audio experience prompt may inspire an artist to create a visual artwork that responds to sound, or vice versa. This can lead to innovative and experimental art forms that blur the boundaries between visual and auditory art.

Creative Coding Prompts

One of the most exciting aspects of AI-generated art prompts is the potential for artists to engage with creative coding. Creative coding involves using programming languages or software to create interactive, dynamic, and generative artworks. AI-generated art prompts can provide artists with coding challenges or code snippets that can serve as a starting point for creating their own unique generative art.

Creative coding prompts can be a gateway for artists to explore the intersection of art, technology, and programming. Artists can experiment with different coding languages, algorithms, or software, and create their own custom generative art that is responsive to various inputs, such as user interaction, data, or external stimuli. This can result in utterly unique and dynamic art forms that evolve and transform in real-time, offering an immersive and interactive experience for viewers.

Additionally, creative coding prompts can also encourage collaboration between artists and technologists, as artists may seek assistance or collaborate with programmers or developers to bring their generative art visions to life. This can foster interdisciplinary collaboration and result in groundbreaking artworks that push the boundaries of traditional art forms and redefine the relationship between art and technology.

Benefits and Challenges of AI-Generated Art Prompts

As with any creative process, there are both benefits and challenges to using AI-generated art prompts. Let us take a closer look at some of these:

Benefits of AI-Generated Art Prompts:

Fresh and Unexpected Inspiration: AI-generated art prompts offer artists a unique source of inspiration that can break free from the confines of traditional prompts. The unpredictable and often unconventional nature of AI-generated prompts can spark new creative directions, ideas, and possibilities that may not have been considered otherwise.

Innovation and Experimentation: AI-generated art prompts encourage artists to push the boundaries of traditional art forms and explore new techniques, mediums, and genres. The fusion of art and technology in AI-generated prompts can lead to innovative and experimental art forms that challenge the status quo and redefine the definition of art.

Access to Cutting-Edge Technology: AI-generated art prompts allow artists to harness the power of advanced technology, such as machine learning algorithms or creative coding, to create unique and interactive artworks. This provides artists with access to innovative tools and techniques that can elevate their artistic practice to new heights.

Multisensory Experiences: AI-generated art prompts often incorporate visual, auditory, and sometimes even other sensory stimuli, providing artists with an opportunity to explore multisensory art forms. This can result in truly immersive and engaging artworks that appeal to a wide range of senses and create a memorable experience for viewers.

Collaborative Opportunities: AI-generated art prompts can foster collaboration between artists and technologists, leading to interdisciplinary partnerships and groundbreaking artworks that combine artistic creativity with technological expertise. This can open new possibilities for artists to collaborate with experts in other fields and create innovative and innovative art.

Challenges of AI-Generated Art Prompts:

Ethical Considerations: The use of AI in art raises ethical considerations, such as questions about the ownership, authorship, and originality of AI-generated art. Artists need to navigate the ethical implications of using AI in their creative process and consider the potential impact on the art world, cultural heritage, and societal values.

Technical Skills and Access to Technology: AI-generated art prompts often require artists to have a certain level of technical skills and access to advanced technology, such as coding or machine learning software. This can pose challenges for artists who may not be familiar with these technologies or have limited access to them, limiting their ability to fully engage with AI-generated prompts.

Balance between Human and AI Creativity: While AI-generated art prompts offer fresh and innovative inspiration, it's essential for artists to strike a balance between human creativity and AI-generated prompts. Overreliance on AI-generated prompts may result in artworks that lack the depth, originality, and personal expression that come from human creativity.

Copyright and Intellectual Property Issues: The use of AI in art raises complex copyright and intellectual property issues, as questions about authorship, ownership, and attribution can arise. Artists need to be mindful of the legal implications of using AI-generated prompts and ensure that they comply with copyright laws and ethical standards.

Bias and Fairness in AI Algorithms: AI algorithms used in generating art prompts may carry biases, as they are trained on large datasets that reflect societal biases. Artists need to be aware of potential biases in AI-generated prompts and consider the ethical implications of using biased algorithms in their creative process.

Tips for Engaging with AI-Generated Art Prompts

To make the most out of AI-generated art prompts, artists can consider the following tips:

Embrace the Unpredictability: AI-generated art prompts are known for their unpredictable nature, and artists can embrace this quality by letting go of preconceived notions and being open to unexpected results. Embrace the uniqueness and novelty of AI-generated prompts as a source of inspiration for your creative process.

Experiment and Innovate: Use AI-generated prompts as an opportunity to experiment with new techniques, mediums, and genres. Push the boundaries of traditional art forms and explore innovative ways to incorporate AI-generated prompts into your artistic practice. Embrace the fusion of art and technology to create groundbreaking artworks that challenge the status quo.

Find the Balance between Human and AI Creativity: Strike a balance between human creativity and AI-generated prompts. Use AI-generated prompts as a tool to enhance your artistic vision, but do not solely rely on them. Infuse your personal expression, ideas, and emotions into your artworks to ensure that they reflect your unique artistic voice.

Consider Ethical Implications: Reflect on the ethical implications of using AI in your creative process. Consider questions about ownership, authorship, originality, copyright, and biases in AI algorithms. Be mindful of ethical standards and comply with copyright laws to ensure that your artwork is ethically and legally sound.

Collaborate and Learn: Engage in collaborative opportunities with experts in other fields, such as technologists, to explore the full potential of AI-generated prompts. Collaborative partnerships can lead to groundbreaking artworks that combine artistic creativity with technological expertise. Also, continue learning and staying updated on advancements in AI and its applications in art to fully leverage the potential of AI-generated prompts.

AI-generated art prompts offer artists a unique source of inspiration that can lead to innovative and experimental artworks. They provide access to innovative technology, foster collaborative opportunities, and open new possibilities for artistic expression. However, artists should be mindful of the ethical considerations, balance between human and AI creativity, and potential biases in AI algorithms. By embracing the unpredictability, experimenting, and finding the right balance, artists can engage with AI-generated art prompts in a way that enhances their artistic practice and leads to groundbreaking artworks that redefine the boundaries of traditional art forms.

preconceived notions and being open to unexpected results. Embrace the uniqueness and novelty of AI-generated prompts as a source of inspiration for your creative process.

Experiment and Innovate: Use AI-generated prompts as an opportunity to experiment with new techniques, mediums, and genres. Push the boundaries of traditional art forms and explore innovative ways to incorporate AI-generated prompts into your artistic practice. Embrace the fusion of art and technology to create groundbreaking artworks that challenge the status quo.

Find the Balance between Human and AI Creativity: Strike a balance between human creativity and AI-generated prompts. Use AI-generated prompts as a tool to enhance your artistic vision, but do not solely rely on them. Infuse your personal expression, ideas, and emotions into your artworks to ensure that they reflect your unique artistic voice.

Consider Ethical Implications: Reflect on the ethical implications of using AI in your creative process. Consider questions about ownership, authorship, originality, copyright, and biases in AI algorithms. Be mindful of ethical standards and comply with copyright laws to ensure that your artwork is ethically and legally sound.

Collaborate and Learn: Engage in collaborative opportunities with experts in other fields, such as technologists, to explore the full potential of AI-generated prompts. Collaborative partnerships can lead to groundbreaking artworks that combine artistic creativity with technological expertise. Also, continue learning and staying updated on advancements in AI and its applications in art to fully leverage the potential of AI-generated prompts.

Conclusion

AI-generated art prompts offer artists a unique source of inspiration that can lead to innovative and experimental artworks. They provide access to innovative technology, foster collaborative opportunities, and open new possibilities for artistic expression. However, artists should be mindful of the ethical considerations, balance between human and AI creativity, and potential biases in AI algorithms. By embracing the unpredictability, experimenting, and finding the right balance, artists can engage with AI-generated art prompts in a way that enhances their artistic practice and leads to groundbreaking artworks that redefine the boundaries of traditional art forms.

Don't miss out!

Visit the website below and you can sign up to receive emails whenever Michael Ferguson publishes a new book. There's no charge and no obligation.

https://books2read.com/r/B-A-CKNW-JKAIC

BOOKS 2 READ

Connecting independent readers to independent writers.

Did you love *Coding Creativity - How to build A Chatbot or Art Generator from Scratch with Bonus: The Ai Prompting Bible*? Then you should read *Artistic Inspiration - The Top 500 "In The Style Of" Ai Art Prompts*[1] by Michael Ferguson!

Artistic Inspiration - The Top 500 "In The Style Of" AI Art Prompts is the ultimate tool for artists seeking to unlock their creativity and push the boundaries of their art. Featuring a curated list of 500 renowned artists, this book leverages the power of AI technology to generate art prompts in the style of these master artists.

Imagine being able to create art in the style of Van Gogh, Monet, Picasso, or any of your favorite artists with just a simple AI-generated prompt. With this book, you have the power to do just that. Each

---

1. https://books2read.com/u/bwy6PO

2. https://books2read.com/u/bwy6PO

artist is carefully selected based on their unique style, genre, and period, ensuring a diverse range of artistic inspirations.

Using the provided AI art prompts, you can experiment with different combinations to create stunning artworks that emulate the styles of these master artists. Whether you are a seasoned artist looking to expand your artistic repertoire or a beginner seeking guidance in finding your own artistic voice, this book provides you with a wealth of inspiration and creative possibilities.

But, like any creative tool, it's important to note that AI art prompts are not a guarantee of perfection. They are meant to be a starting point for your own creative exploration. Experimentation, iteration, and personalization are key to truly making the art your own. Before you start, we recommend testing out different prompts, tweaking and refining them to suit your unique artistic vision.

Artistic Inspiration - The Top 500 "In The Style Of" AI Art Prompts is not just a book, but a creative journey that empowers you to unlock your artistic potential, expand your artistic horizons, and elevate your art to new heights. Let the power of AI and the wisdom of master artists guide and inspire you on your creative path. Join the AI art revolution and #UnlockYourCreativity today!